CORETTA SCOTT KING

CORETTA SCOTT KING

A Biography

Laura T. McCarty

GREENWOOD BIOGRAPHIES

GREENWOOD PRESS
WESTPORT, CONNECTICUT • LONDON

Library of Congress Cataloging-in-Publication Data

McCarty, Laura T.
  Coretta Scott King : a biography / Laura T. McCarty.
    p. cm. — (Greenwood biographies, ISSN 1540–4900)
  Includes bibliographical references and index.
  ISBN 978–0–313–34981–2 (alk. paper)
  1. King, Coretta Scott, 1927–2006. 2. African American women civil rights
workers—Biography. 3. Civil rights workers—United States—Biography. 4. African
Americans—Biography. 5. King, Martin Luther, Jr., 1929–1968. 6. African
Americans—Civil rights—History—20th century. 7. Civil rights movements—United
States—History—20th century. I. Title.
  E185.97.K47M387 2009
  323.092—dc22 [B]   2009005809

British Library Cataloguing in Publication Data is available.

Library of Congress Catalog Card Number: 2009005809

ISBN: 978–0–313–34981–2
ISSN: 1540–4900

First published in 2009

Greenwood Press, 88 Post Road West, Westport, CT 06881
An imprint of Greenwood Publishing Group, Inc.
www.greenwood.com

Printed in the United States of America

The paper used in this book complies with the
Permanent Paper Standard issued by the National
Information Standards Organization (Z39.48–1984).

10 9 8 7 6 5 4 3 2 1

CONTENTS

Photo essay follows page 90

SERIES FOREWORD

In response to high school and public library needs, Greenwood developed this distinguished series of full-length biographies specifically for student use. Prepared by field experts and professionals, these engaging biographies are tailored for high school students who need challenging yet accessible biographies. Ideal for secondary school assignments, the length, format, and subject areas are designed to meet educators' requirements and students' interests.

Greenwood offers an extensive selection of biographies spanning all curriculum-related subject areas including social studies, the sciences, literature and the arts, history and politics, as well as popular culture, covering public figures and famous personalities from all time periods and backgrounds, both historic and contemporary, who have made an impact on American and/or world culture. Greenwood biographies were chosen based on comprehensive feedback from librarians and educators. Consideration was given to both curriculum relevance and inherent interest. The result is an intriguing mix of the well known and the unexpected, the saints and sinners from long-ago history and contemporary pop culture. Readers will find a wide array of subject choices from fascinating crime figures like Al Capone to inspiring pioneers like Margaret Mead, from the greatest minds of our time like Stephen Hawking to the most amazing success stories of our day like J. K. Rowling.

While the emphasis is on fact, not glorification, the books are meant to be fun to read. Each volume provides in-depth information about the subject's life from birth through childhood, the teen years, and adulthood. A thorough account relates family background and education, traces personal and professional influences, and explores struggles, accomplishments, and contributions. A timeline highlights the most significant life events against a historical perspective. Bibliographies supplement the reference value of each volume.

ACKNOWLEDGMENTS

My interest in Coretta Scott King grew out of writing an article on her life for the *New Georgia Encyclopedia* (www.georgiaencyclopedia.org). I thank the editors John Inscoe and Kelly Caudle for giving me that initial opportunity to learn more about this interesting and brave woman. I also thank Sandy Towers at Greenwood for the opportunity to expand the article into a full-length biography.

I thank the board and staff of the Georgia Humanities Council, especially president Jamil Zainaldin, for their support. I also thank historians Vicki Crawford, Glenn Eskew, Mary Gambrell Rolinson, Glenn Robins, and Mary Evelyn Tomlin for suggestions and encouragement.

Last, but not least, special thanks go to my husband, Phillip, for putting up with my filling our guest room with research materials and for letting me take the laptop on vacation with us. I also thank my sisters Rebecca and Mary Jane for their ongoing love and support.

TIMELINE: EVENTS IN THE LIFE OF CORETTA SCOTT KING

April 27, 1927	Born in Perry County, Alabama, the daughter of Obadiah and Bernice McMurray Scott.
1933–1939	Attends Crossroads School, a rural one-room school.
1939–1945	Attends Lincoln High School, a semiprivate school in Marion.
1945	Graduates from Lincoln High School as valedictorian.
1945–1951	Attends and graduates from Antioch College, Yellow Springs, Ohio; majors in music and education.
1951–1954	Attends and graduates from New England Conservatory of Music in Boston.
1952	Meets Martin Luther King, Jr.
June 18, 1953	Marries Martin Luther King, Jr., on the porch of her parents' home in Alabama. "Daddy" King, her husband's father, conducts the service.
1954	Moves to Montgomery, Alabama, where Martin becomes pastor of Dexter Avenue Baptist Church.
November 17, 1955	First daughter, Yolanda Denise, is born.
December 1–5	Rosa Parks is arrested; the Montgomery Improvement Association is formed, with Martin as leader; Montgomery Bus Boycott begins; Coretta arranges for taping of Martin's speeches.

January 30, 1956	King parsonage is bombed.
November	U.S. Supreme Court issues ruling in *Browder v. Gayle*, which ends the Montgomery Bus Boycott.
December 5	Performs during a concert in Manhattan to raise funds for the Montgomery Improvement Association.
January 1957	Attends meeting to form Southern Christian Leadership Conference (SCLC); presides for Martin when he has to return to Montgomery due to a bombing at the home of Ralph David Abernathy.
March	Travels to Ghana to attend the celebration of its establishment as an independent nation.
October 23	Martin Luther King III is born.
Spring 1958	Makes her public speaking debut at the New Hope Baptist Church in Denver.
October	Speaks at Youth March and Rally for Desegregation at the Lincoln Memorial in Washington, D.C., while Martin is recovering from stab wounds.
February 1959	Travels to India with Martin to learn about Gandhi. Joins Women's International League for Peace and Freedom.
November	Martin resigns as pastor of Dexter Avenue Baptist Church to become copastor of Ebenezer Baptist; the family moves to Atlanta.
February 1960	Serves as delegate to White House Conference on Children and Youth.
May	Martin is arrested for driving with an expired license while carrying author Lillian Smith (*Strange Fruit*, 1944) back to the hospital for cancer treatments; Coretta is also in the car. Martin receives a suspended sentence. After another arrest, as a result of a march with the Atlanta Student Movement, Martin is jailed in DeKalb County, Georgia, and then is transferred to the state prison in Reidsville. Coretta asks for help from members of the John F. Kennedy campaign, which leads to John F. Kennedy's and Robert Kennedy's intervention in the case.
January 3, 1961	Dexter Scott King is born.

April 1962	Serves as delegate for the Women's Strike for Peace Conference in Geneva, Switzerland.
Summer	The Albany Movement—Coretta attends protests, speaks to crowds, and visits Martin in jail.
March 28, 1963	Bernice Albertine King is born.
April	Birmingham Campaign; Coretta visits Martin in jail.
April 18	Suggests to Martin that he call for a March on Washington.
August 28	Attends March on Washington; sits on the stage during Martin's "I Have a Dream" speech.
1964–1966	Conducts a series of Freedom Concerts, fundraisers for the SCLC.
1964	Martin receives Nobel Peace Prize; Coretta accompanies him to Norway to accept prize; participates, with children, in dinner to honor him at the Dinkler Hotel in Atlanta.
February 1965	Attends mass meeting in Selma, Alabama; gives speech and meets Malcolm X.
March	Participates in sections of the Selma to Montgomery March; performs as part of the concert the last night of the march at the City of Hope complex on the outskirts of Montgomery.
June 8	Speaks at Emergency Peace Rally, Madison Square Garden, New York City.
August	Registers Yolanda and Martin III at Spring Street Elementary in Atlanta, part of the desegregation of the Atlanta Public Schools.
1966	Moves with Martin and children to apartment in Chicago during the Chicago Movement.
June	With Martin and three of her children, participates in the James Meredith March against Fear in Mississippi.
July	Serves as a delegate to the White House conference, "To Fulfill These Rights."
April 15, 1967	Speaks at Spring Mobilization against War in San Francisco.
January 15, 1968	Participates in the Women's Peace Brigade March, led by Jeannette Rankin, in Washington, D.C.
January	Has surgery for a tumor in her abdomen.

March	Participates in press conference about plans for the Poor People's Campaign.
April 4	Martin is assassinated in Memphis.
April 6	Makes statement to the press about Martin's death.
April 8	Returns to Memphis to march with striking sanitation workers; makes speech about continuing Martin's work.
April 9	Martin's funeral.
April 11	Meets with Atlanta Mayor Ivan Allen about the establishment of a memorial in Atlanta.
April 27	Speaks at peace rally in Central Park, New York City.
May	Leads Mother's Day March for Welfare Rights and gives keynote speech.
June	Gives keynote address at Harvard University; the first woman to speak at a Harvard graduation.
June 19	Featured speaker at the Poor People's Campaign, calls for women to mobilize against "triple evils" of poverty, racism, and war.
June 26	The King Center is incorporated.
July	Speaks at press conference to announce plans for first annual Martin Luther King, Jr., Birthday Celebration.
	Goes into seclusion in New Hampshire to write autobiography.
July 23	Gives keynote speech at Women: Power in Action: Towards the Reduction of Violence conference, sponsored by *McCall's* magazine.
Fall	Launches Library Documentation Project of the King Center.
January 1969	Visits Italy; is first African American recipient of the Universal Love award from the Italian government. Visits India; accepts posthumous presentation of the Nehru Humanitarian Award to Martin.
March 17	Speaks at St. Paul's Cathedral in London; the first woman to do so.
March	Receives honorary doctorate from Boston University. Participates in SCLC demonstrations in Charleston, South Carolina, that leads to the formation of a union at hospitals there.

June   Receives first Frances Blanchard Fellowship at Yale.

September *My Life with Martin Luther King, Jr.* is published.

November   Receives Pacem in Terra award from the International Overseas Foundation. Receives the Eleanor Roosevelt Award from Society Against Nuclear Energy.

January 1970 First meeting of the King Center Board of Directors; formation of the Institute for the Black World, housed at the Atlanta University Center.

1970   Travels to Europe on book tour; performs Freedom Concert in Amsterdam. Authorizes filmmaker Eli Landau to develop documentary *King: A Filmed Record from Montgomery to Memphis*. Receives honorary degrees from Princeton and Harvard.

1971   The King Center conducts first conference on nonviolence and publishes a report. The King Center also conducts two projects: "Violence in the Schools" and "The Socialization of Blacks in White Universities."

1972   The King Center is renamed the Martin Luther King, Jr. Center for Nonviolent Social Change. The King Center receives grant from the National Institutes of Health to study violence in factories.

1972–1984 Appointed to the Planning Commission on Presidential Elections.

1973   The King Center presents first Martin Luther King, Jr. Nonviolent Peace Prize to Andrew Young. The U.S. Department of Housing and Urban Development awards a $2.8 million grant toward the development of the King Community Center and Park. Alpha Kappa Alpha Sorority provides funds for the acquisition and restoration of the King Birth Home. Coretta works to get land on Auburn Avenue declared as a National Historic Site. The King Center hosts its first oral history conference.

1974   The King Center presents a Nonviolent Peace Prize to César Chávez.

June 18	Cofounds the National Committee for Full Employment.
Summer	Launches fundraising effort for the Freedom Hall complex.
January 1975	The King Center hosts a policy conference on the Voting Rights Act of 1965. The King Birth Home is dedicated. Coretta and three of her children visit Africa.
January 1976	The King Center hosts first annual Labor Management Social Responsibility Breakfast. King Day March festivities include a March for Full Employment. Coretta participates in the dedication of the King Community Center and Early Learning Center.
Summer	The King Center conducts summer institute on nonviolence in partnership with the National Education Association.
1977	King Birthday commemorative service becomes interfaith. Phase III of the King Center Complex is dedicated. The King Center receives a National Endowment for the Humanities grant to preserve and catalog the papers of Martin and the SCLC. Ebenezer Baptist Church, the Birth Home, and the King Center are named National Landmarks.
Fall	Appointed public delegate to the United Nations by President Jimmy Carter; cochairs Full Employment Week; cofounds the Black Leadership Forum and the Black Leadership Roundtable.
November 21	Participates in the National Women's Conference and makes recommendations to Congress and the President about women's status.
1978	President Jimmy Carter hosts a reception for Friends of the King Center at the White House; Coretta performs a portion of the Freedom Concert. Coretta is appointed as Deputy Chair for the White House Conference on Families.
May 23	Meets with President Carter on behalf of the Comprehensive Education and Training Act (CETA).
August 18	Meets with President Carter about the Humphrey-Hawkins Bill.

Fall	Lobbies to extend the deadline to ratify the Equal Rights Amendment.
October 1979	Groundbreaking for the Freedom Hall museum at the King Center.
1980	Congress enacts and President Carter signs law establishing the Martin Luther King Historic Site and Preservation District.
May	Receives the Outstanding Mother Award from the National Mothers' Day Committee.
June 13	Addresses the Hispanic Leadership Conference in Houston.
August	Speaks at the Democratic National Convention to second the nomination of President Jimmy Carter.
1981	Addresses disarmament rally in Bonn, Germany. The King Center moves its administrative offices to Auburn Avenue.
June 23	Testifies on voting rights enforcement before the House Judiciary Committee, Subcommittee on Civil and Constitutional Rights.
August 11	Speaks at International Day of Solidarity with South Africa Rally.
October	The King Center archives are opened for research.
1982	Freedom Hall is dedicated. Travels to Panama to dedicate a housing project named for Martin. Receives honorary doctorate from Antioch College.
June 9	Speaks at World Peace March calling for the United Nations to have a special session on disarmament.
December 10	Hosts international conference at the King Center on Central America and the Caribbean Basin.
1983	Works with committee to commemorate the twentieth anniversary of the March on Washington.
September	Meets with Indira Gandhi.
October 2	Initiates annual Gandhi Birthday celebration at the King Center; dedicates a room in Freedom Hall to Gandhi.
November 2	President Ronald Reagan signs bill establishing Martin Luther King, Jr.'s birthday as a federal holiday.

1984 Receives the Cross of Legion from France's President François Mitterand. Receives honorary degree from Spelman College. Named National Treasure by *Family Weekly* magazine. Leads delegation to Zimbabwe for United Nations Decade of Women Conference.

1985 Establishes Martin Luther King, Jr. Papers Project. Presents Martin Luther King, Jr. Peace Prize to Bishop Tutu of South Africa.

May 14 Participates in protest to call for freedom in South Africa.

July Arrested with Martin III and Bernice while protesting apartheid at the South African Embassy.

August Participates with President Reagan at signing for Civil Rights Act of 1985.

January 1986 First national Martin Luther King, Jr. holiday celebrated.

Leads goodwill mission to Japan. Publishes article to protest the death penalty in Michigan.

May Meets with Mubarak Awad, founder of the Palestinian Center for Nonviolence. Leads King Center group to South Africa. Participates in Peace and Freedom Walk in the Philippines, invited by Philippine president Corazon Aquino.

July 4 Receives Ellis Island Medal of Honor as part of the celebration of the 100th anniversary of the Statue of Liberty.

1987 Files lawsuit against Boston University seeking return of Martin's papers.

January Organizes and leads March against Fear and Intimidation in Forsyth County, Georgia. Endorses the Fund for a Feminist Majority.

July Speaks out against President Reagan's nomination of Judge Robert Bork to the U.S. Supreme Court.

1988 Receives award from the President of Gabon. Speaks to United Nations Disarmament Rally in New York. Endorses the Women's Peace Platform and presents it to the United Nations. Testifies before the Republican platform committee. Co-convenes the 25th anniversary of the March on

	Washington. Serves as a delegate to the conference Women for Meaningful Change held in Athens, Greece. Cohosts Trailblazers and Torch Bearers: Women in the Civil Rights Movement conference at Georgia State University.
1989	Participates in the march Women's Equality, Women's Lives, hosted by the National Organization for Women.
January 15	Resigns as president of the King Center and announces that Dexter will assume this role.
April 5	Dexter becomes president of the King Center.
August 17	Dexter resigns from presidency of King Center. Coretta remains CEO and spokeswoman.
September	Issues statement of solidarity with South African women.
October	Participates in the National March for Housing Now in Washington, D.C. Meets with President Bush and Vice President Quayle.
January 13, 1990	The King Center debuts 400-page teaching guide about Martin's life and philosophy.
1990	Coconvenes Soviet-American Women's Summit. Participates in the 25th anniversary of the Selma to Montgomery March. Meets with Secretary of State James Baker. Serves on the Leadership Council for Earth Day. Serves as Chairperson for Atlanta Committee to Host Tribute to Nelson and Winnie Mandela.
1991	Speaks out against the bombing of Iraq. Attends African-American Summit in the Ivory Coast. Participates in the 10th anniversary celebration of independence in Zimbabwe. Writes a version of her autobiography for young readers.
January 18, 1993	Calls for March on Washington to commemorate 30th anniversary of Martin's "I Have a Dream" speech.
April 4	Marks 25th anniversary of Martin's assassination.
April 26	Testifies in trial in lawsuit over Martin's papers.
April 30	Attends "Tribute to Coretta Scott King" fundraiser for The King Center on the occasion of her 66th birthday.

January 16, 2000	Federal funds are appropriated to restore Ebenezer Baptist Church.
June 10	The Department of Justice concludes investigation of Martin's assassination and finds no evidence of conspiracy.
October 19	Marks 20th anniversary of Martin Luther King, Jr. Historic Site.
January 21, 2002	First Lady Laura Bush attends Commemorative Service for King Holiday.
April 27	Celebrates 75th birthday.
May 5, 2003	Appears on Oprah Winfrey television program to show off an "Age Defying Makeover."
November 17	Dexter announces his resignation from the King Center and Martin III's appointment as new CEO. Coretta temporarily agrees to become Chairman again.
January 15, 2004	President George W. Bush visits to lay a wreath on Martin's grave, in conjunction with what would have been his 75th birthday.
Fall	Moves into a penthouse condominium in Buckhead (an Atlanta neighborhood).
December 11	Bernice King participates in march led by Bishop Eddie Long, one of the goals of which is to protest same-sex marriage.
January 17, 2005	Tavis Smiley broadcasts what would become Coretta's last media interview, from Ebenezer Baptist Church.
April 26	Hospitalized due to atrial fibrillation.
August 16	Suffers major stroke.
December	Media reports indicate dispute among King siblings regarding the future of the King Center.
January 14, 2006	Makes last public appearance at Salute to Greatness dinner.
January 30	Dies of ovarian cancer and after effects from stroke at holistic health center in Mexico.
February 7	Funeral at New Birth Missionary Baptist Church.
November 20	Family dedicates new crypt at King Center.

INTRODUCTION

Coretta Scott King is known and remembered as the wife and widow of
Dr. Martin Luther King, Jr. She is one of the iconic widows from the
1960s, one whose image is associated with those of Jacqueline Kennedy,
Betty Shabazz (widow of Malcolm X), and Myrlie Evers (widow of mur-
dered activist Medgar Evers).[1]

To the Southern Christian Leadership Conference (SCLC)/Women's
Organizational Movement for Equality Now, Inc., which placed a marker
to Coretta beside her home church in Alabama, she is also the "First Lady
of the Civil Rights Movement."[2] This title is certainly justifiable, as Martin Luther King, Jr., was one of the founders and the first president of the
SCLC, an organization that was central to the battles toward the integration of transportation, restaurants, and businesses as well as toward
obtaining voting rights for African Americans.

But who was Coretta Scott King in her own right? Since her death
in 2006, scholars have begun to work toward understanding her life and
work in full historical context.[3]

Undoubtedly, as additional archival collections are organized and
opened for research, the answers to this question will proliferate.

Meanwhile, here is the outline of her life: She was a daughter of rural
Alabama who went to college in the North and later returned to live in
the urban South. She was a singer and a lover of music as well as a reader
and a thinker. Inspired by strong Christian faith, she worked for a peaceful
and just society.

Once she met Martin Luther King, Jr., she was an important helpmate
in his work in the church and in the civil rights movement. She was

poised and graceful, which contributed to her success as a Baptist minister's wife. She also served as the primary caretaker of their four children and the manager of their household affairs. Responsibilities at home kept her from being on the frontlines of the civil rights efforts daily, yet she did manage to participate in a number of key occasions. Even when she was not able to participate, she served as a listening ear and sounding board, a confidante for her husband's thoughts and fears.

Coretta Scott King loved Martin Luther King, Jr., and supported him following his call in life. From behind the scenes, she made provisions to preserve the body of his thoughts, from typing his dissertation to audio-recording his sermons. When difficult days arose or violence threatened, she managed to remain calm, and these steady reactions helped Martin: They manifested the character of nonviolence.

After Martin's death, Coretta sought to continue his work and to memorialize his life through establishing the Martin Luther King, Jr. Center for Nonviolent Social Change and the Martin Luther King, Jr. Federal Holiday (the first such holiday to honor an individual person of color). She worked tirelessly to build and raise support for these institutions, through which she continued to make a difference in the world. The three-block complex that grew up around Martin's grave and church has become one of the most visited tourist attractions in Atlanta. The King Holiday also is celebrated across the United States and around the world.

Coretta was also a promoter and spokesperson for nonviolence and peace and justice issues in her own right. She was concerned about national and international issues. In addition, she advocated for equality for all persons and for the end of discrimination due to any reason: race, gender, religion, ethnicity, sexual orientation, disability status, or income level. In short, she was a very active and busy person, and as she promoted her husband's legacy in so many ways, she also created legacies of her own.

A group of librarians—and ultimately the American Library Association—chose her as the namesake of the Coretta Scott King Awards, which honor authors and illustrators of color for producing books that promote understanding and appreciation of African American culture and of the contributions of all people to the achievement of the American dream. The awards have been presented since 1969. The works of the honored authors and illustrators have collectively and individually passed on significant information about history and culture to a mass of young readers, including the values of peace, brotherhood, and nonviolent social change.

In a speech in 2004 at Antioch College, her alma mater, Coretta revealed a core commitment that explained how she connected all of the various aspects of her existence: "I have always felt that it is important to integrate all aspects of one's life into a harmonious whole, instead of compartmentalizing the roles that we are called to play in life."[4] Another core commitment was her Christian faith, which maintains that through sacrificial love, justice prevails.

The story of Coretta Scott King's life manifests these two core beliefs. While it was occasionally difficult for Coretta to make others understand how all of her activities and statements fit together, she always felt that she was consistent. She will be remembered as a person who kept faith and worked toward making the world a better place.

NOTES

1. Michael Eric Dyson, *Why I Love Black Women* (New York: Basic Civitas Books, 2003), 73.

2. Coretta Scott King Monument, Mt. Tabor AME Zion Church, Perry County, Alabama.

3. Vicki Crawford, "In Memoriam: Coretta Scott King and the Struggle for Civil and Human Rights: An Enduring Legacy," *The Journal of African American History* 92:1 (January 2007): 106.

4. Coretta Scott King, "Address by Coretta Scott King: Antioch Reunion 2004," *The Antiochian: The Newsletter of Antioch College,* Fall 2004, http://www.antioch-college.edu/news/csk/2004Mannacceptance.html.

Chapter 1

BLACK BELT HERITAGE

Coretta Scott was born on April 27, 1927, in an unincorporated area in north central Perry County, Alabama, approximately 12 miles from the county seat of Marion. Coretta's parents were Bernice McMurray Scott and Obadiah "Obie" Scott. Coretta was the family's middle child, arriving between Edythe (born December 13, 1924) and Obie Leonard (born April 22, 1930). Another child, Eunice, had died as a four-year-old prior to Edythe's birth.

THE BLACK BELT

Perry County lies on land acquired from the Creek Indians in the 1814 Treaty of Fort Jackson. Early pioneers came from the Carolinas, Georgia, and Tennessee, anxious to farm the rich soil of the area.[1] Their prime crop was cotton, as it continued to be until the early twentieth century. The early settlers brought with them enslaved Africans who cleared the land for fields and were vital to the cultivation of cotton. Because of this heritage of cotton and farming, this part of Alabama is called the "Black Belt."[2]

The Emancipation Proclamation and the conclusion of the Civil War provided for the end of slavery for these people. Many of them continued to live and develop their own community institutions in the same areas where they had been enslaved.

While the Civil War had brought the promise of freedom, Reconstruction marked a return to the ways of white supremacy and segregation by law and by custom. U.S. Supreme Court decisions, such as *Plessy v.*

Ferguson (1896), upheld segregation of schools and other public accommodations. States also enacted poll taxes and literacy tests that were designed to keep African Americans from voting. In addition, white intimidation and violence stifled any possibility of resistance by African Americans. The 1901 Alabama state constitution made it illegal for African Americans to vote. Strangely enough, the majority of votes to pass this Constitution came from counties in the Black Belt, where African Americans made up the vast majority of the population. As a result of fraud and intimidation, the few African Americans who were registered to vote at this time appeared to join white citizens in voting in favor of their own disfranchisement.[3]

Perry County was an example of what scholars call Jim Crow Society. *Jim Crow* was the name of a character in a minstrel show created by a white man, Thomas "Daddy" Rice, in the early nineteenth century. By mid-century, the character became standard in minstrel shows, one of the stereotypical, negative depictions of African Americans common to that era. In addition, in 1841, there is documentation of the term as applying to segregated rail cars in the North. While the exact path of the spread of the term is unknown, by the 1880s, "Jim Crow had become synonymous with a complex system of racial laws and customs in the South that ensured white social, legal, and political domination of blacks."[4] African Americans were unable to vote and attended poorly equipped and poorly funded schools. Signs labeled "white" and "colored" designated which water fountains, entrances, restrooms, or waiting areas people were allowed to use.

In rural areas, many African Americans were sharecroppers, working on farms owned by whites. The landowner would provide seed and fertilizer in exchange for receiving a share of the crop raised. The tenants also obtained household supplies or farm materials through credit provided by the landowner's store. This system, as well as the contingencies of weather and harvest production, often kept the workers in perpetual debt to the owners.

By the early twentieth century, soil erosion and the boll weevil had led to a decline in cotton production in Perry County. While some cotton fields remained, others had been abandoned to timber forests. Still, agriculture remained a center of the rural economy.

FAMILY

In spite of the horrors of Jim Crow segregation, "many African Americans created meaningful lives by developing institutions within their own communities, and black churches, schools, businesses, and other institutions flourished."[5] Coretta's family members were leaders in their rural community, intimately connected to the networks of church, school, and land. From this heritage, Coretta gained many of her lifelong values and principles about life. She also learned to value mutual aid and community involvement as keys to individual success.

Coretta's maternal grandfather was Martin McMurray, who was part Native American. Mr. McMurray lived on a farm in the area. He did not own a car, and he rarely ventured outside of the county. Although he had not had an opportunity to attend school for long during his childhood, he could read and developed a large vocabulary through studying biblical reference works. He was one of the worship leaders at Mount Tabor African Methodist Episcopal Zion Church, the family's house of worship.

Coretta's paternal grandfather was Jeff Scott, and Obadiah Scott was one of 13 children born to Jeff and Cora Scott. After the Civil War, Jeff and Cora worked and acquired a farm, which eventually occupied 300 acres. After Cora's death, Jeff married Fannie Burroughs, who gave birth to 12 children. It was this large extended family that made up the majority of the community into which Coretta was born.

Coretta's parents lived in a two-room house, surrounded by pine thickets, off a dirt road. A wood-burning stove provided the heat and cooking space. The central pieces of furniture were a kitchen table and chairs. However, the family also had an old wind-up Victrola record player, a collection of records, and a few books. Coretta's mother loved to listen to the blues singer Bessie Smith.

WORK

In 1929, the U.S. stock market crashed, plunging the country into the Great Depression. While economic conditions in the rural South had been difficult previously, the Depression intensified the hard times. All of the Scott family had to work together in order to make ends meet. In addition, rural families often assisted each other by sharing work or food provisions when times were particularly tough.

By the time she was six or seven and could hold a hoe, Coretta joined her parents and her siblings in working on their farm, raising corn, potatoes, peas, and garden vegetables. The farm produced food for the family and their animals. The children were also responsible for feeding the cows and chickens.

At age 10, Coretta began to work in the cotton fields with a group of hired hands, hoeing and chopping in the summer and picking in the fall. As a young teenager, she went to work for another farmer, picking cotton to earn money for school. Family lore has it that she once picked 200 pounds of cotton in a single day, earning $7.00, a large amount for a single day's effort. In addition, she claimed to consistently pick more cotton than her male cousins.

FAITH COMMUNITY

Besides providing for the family land, Coretta's forefathers established a tradition of leadership that carried forth into successive generations. Jeff Scott held central roles in Mount Tabor Church and served as an officer for the Rising Star Burial Society. Because of these civic commitments, he traveled frequently to conferences and gained perspectives on the issues that were facing African Americans beyond rural Perry County. Organizations like the Rising Star provided mutual aid to African Americans across the rural and urban South, and they were also a business network, via selling insurance policies.

Mount Tabor Church was the center of social life for the African American community. Families dressed up and walked in or rode in wagons each Sunday. For Coretta's family, it was a four-mile round trip.

The congregation could only afford to hire a minister for two Sundays a month. Therefore, on the first and third Sundays of each month, church members provided the leadership. With a baritone voice, Grandfather McMurray led hymns for the congregation. He would sing a line of the song, which the congregation would then repeat with him. (This style of conducting is called "lining out" a hymn.) Grandfather Scott also led the services, prayed, and read from the Bible.

An important part of Sunday school was instruction in the Catechism. Leaders would ask questions such as "Who is God?" and "What can God do?," and the audience would respond with predetermined statements such as "God is a spirit" and "God can do everything." This method of teaching theology dates back to one that was developed for the instruction of slaves, when slaves were not allowed to be taught to read and write.

Obie Scott served as the Chairman of the Trustees for Mount Tabor, and Bernice Scott was a deaconess, stewardess, and pianist. By the time Coretta was 15, she began to direct the youth choir, in which she and her siblings sang.

In her autobiography, *My Life with Martin Luther King, Jr.*, Coretta remembered the part-time ministers as well-meaning, if poorly educated and ill-prepared to serve the political and economic needs of their people. The ministers' sermons didn't address directly the social and political issues of the day, though they alluded to Bible stories to raise hope and confidence in God's love and providence for his people. Owing to the strong prevalence of white supremacy in Perry County, to openly discuss civil rights or to criticize segregation would have endangered the ministers and their congregations. Yet, the churches, which were Black-owned and Black-led, provided a basis for the community empowerment approach that her generation would take during the civil rights movement.

Growing up in the church also influenced Coretta's commitment to peace and justice issues. She stated that it was "my faith that first made me a good candidate for pacifism."[6]

EDUCATION

Coretta and her siblings began their educations at a one-room school located at a crossroads four miles from their home. The two teachers had junior college educations. The school and its furniture had been built by members of the community, as the county and state did not provide sufficient resources for the education of African Americans. The school met for seven months a year, and it was here, beginning in 1933, that Coretta started to learn about African American history. She also cultivated her interest in music. In her autobiography she fondly remembers a teacher, Ms. Mattie Bennett, who encouraged her and challenged her to learn more.

After completing elementary school in 1939, Coretta continued her education at Lincoln, a private school in Marion whose student body was all African American. Nine ex-slaves opened Lincoln (named after Abraham Lincoln) in 1867, and in 1868, they entered into a partnership with the American Missionary Association, which brought in teachers from the North. In 1874, the State of Alabama took over the school and expanded it to a normal school (a college to train teachers). In 1887, after a fire, the normal school was moved to Montgomery, where it became Alabama State College.[7] In an ironic twist, it was faculty and staff from Alabama State who made up much of the membership of Dexter Avenue Baptist Church, which was the first church that Martin Luther King, Jr., served after his marriage to Coretta.

Even after the departure of the college, the people of Marion and Perry County struggled to keep the high school open. The school maintained a tradition of service to the community, the value of which it instilled in its students. Obie Scott, who had a sixth-grade education, attended Lincoln for one year during his teenaged years. This exposure made him and Bernice more determined that their daughters have every opportunity to pursue their educations and to complete high school. In the early 1940s, tuition for Lincoln was $4.50 per child.

When Edythe and Coretta first began as students at Lincoln, they boarded with a family in Marion because their home was 10 miles away, and the county did not provide transportation for African American students. This was another fee that Obie and Bernice had to cover. When Coretta was in the eleventh grade, the situation changed. Through the advocacy of her parents, the county agreed to provide partial funding toward a bus for the African American students. Coretta's father converted a timber truck into a bus, and Coretta's mother agreed to drive the bus, completing a 40-mile circuit each day.

At Lincoln, Coretta's learning continued. The faculty of Lincoln was integrated, although all but one of the white teachers were from the North, and the teachers lived in integrated dorms on campus. Most of the white community in Marion thought that this arrangement was scandalous, and they suspected the northern whites of being radical in their politics.

The curriculum at Lincoln was rigorous, and the instruction was thorough. The school had a tradition of alumni pursuing college, graduate degrees, and professional training. Guest speakers also often visited to present additional opportunities to the students. Years later, when the civil rights movement organizer Bayard Rustin came to Montgomery to meet and work with Martin during the 1955–1956 bus boycott, Coretta could report that she had met him during her student days at Lincoln.

Classmates described Coretta as warm, talented, slightly reserved, and brilliant. A Lincoln alumnus, Ritten Lee (class of 1943), recalled that when Coretta was in high school, "she was concerned about ideas and philosophy. She was on a higher plane than most of the people her age."[8]

Miss Olive J. Williams, the music teacher, was another particularly strong influence. Miss Williams emphasized the study of classical music. While the inspiration to sing had come from her mother and grandfather McMurray, Miss Williams gave Coretta her first formal voice lessons. Coretta also played the flutaphone and piano. As a teenager, she became the pianist and choir director for her family's church. Coretta's sister recalled, "My sister always sang. All of us sang—my mother sang, we sang together in choirs, in church, in school."[9]

In her autobiography, Coretta credited attending Lincoln as being one of the most significant experiences of her youth. The role models that she met there and the values they instilled in her, she thought, had helped to prepare her for the experiences she would have in later life as the wife of Martin Luther King, Jr.

ROLE MODELS

Another strong influence on Coretta was her mother, Bernice, who had a fourth-grade education. Bernice was shy and reserved, but her actions, such as her willingness to drive the school bus, manifested her internal strength and quiet determination.

Bernice always told her daughters, "You are just as good as anyone else . . . you get an education and try to be somebody. Then, you won't have to be kicked around by anybody and you won't have to depend on anyone for your livelihood, not even on a man."[10] While Bernice spent most of her life serving as a homemaker, she was independent and ready to do whatever it took to make a way for those she loved. Coretta undoubtedly remembered this advice during her marriage to Martin and after his death.

In downtown Marion, Coretta was exposed more to the realities of segregation and racial oppression than she had been while living on her parents' farm. White teenagers expected African Americans to leave the sidewalk if they met there. Coretta worked briefly for a white woman as a domestic, but the job did not last long because Coretta refused to observe the racial etiquette that her employer demanded.

Back in the country, Coretta's father faced his own struggles with white neighbors. In 1937, Obie and family moved into a larger home, which they rented. In 1942, the family's home burned under suspicious circumstances. Local authorities did not investigate, saying that the house was outside the city limits and not within their jurisdiction. When Obie purchased a sawmill, he was pressured to sell it. After he refused, that structure, too, burned. Yet, Obie continued to work, to haul timber, and to provide for his family.

Throughout Coretta's youth, her father held a variety of jobs. He was a barber, a farmer, and a hauler of lumber. He was one of the first African Americans to own a truck in Perry County. Coretta recalled that her father always emphasized to his children the need to keep busy: "If you don't have anything to do, then just get up and sit down."[11] Eventually he set up a grocery store, offering an alternative to the white-owned stores that landowners used to keep tenant farmers constantly in debt. He also built a roomy three-bedroom house adjacent to his store, which still stands. Coretta and Martin were married on the porch of that home.

While serving as a pillar of the rural African American community, Obie also set an example of how to negotiate the rigid color line. Physically, he was only five foot seven. He carried a pistol in his truck, and he worried about what might happen when he would set off at night to work. Yet, he maintained a calm, steady presence, no matter what the circumstances. He told his family, "If you look a white man in the eye, he can't hurt you." Later in life, he reflected, "Nobody hates me. I have paid all of my debts. My credit is good. That is because of the way I have conducted myself. I don't have an enemy in the world."[12] Obie's confidence and calm nature undoubtedly influenced Coretta when she encountered resistance during her life.

This combination of family, land, work, faith, and schooling built a strong foundation for Coretta and led her to develop convictions that she would pursue for the rest of her life. Coretta's roots taught her about poverty and hard work, but they also fostered her belief in herself and her community as well as her commitment to the betterment of broader humankind. She became a strong, independent woman because of the influences of her parents, the church, and the segregated, rural African American community in which she grew up.

NOTES

1. Donna Siebenthaler, "Perry County," *The Encyclopedia of Alabama*, http://www.eoa.auburn.edu/face/ArticlePrintable.jsp?id+h-1292.

2. Allen Tulos, "The Black Belt," *Southern Spaces: An Internet Journal and Scholarly Forum*, http://www.southernspaces.org/contents/2004/tullos/print/4a.htm.

3. William Warren Rogers and Robert David Ward, *Alabama: The History of a Deep South State* (Tuscaloosa: University of Alabama Press, 1994), 343–354.

4. Richard Wormser, *The Rise and Fall of Jim Crow* (New York: St. Martin's Press, 2003), xi.

5. Vicki Crawford, "In Memoriam: Coretta Scott King and the Struggle for Civil and Human Rights: An Enduring Legacy," *The Journal of African American History* 92:1 (January 2007): 106.

6. Mae Gentry, "In the Words of Coretta King," *Atlanta Constitution*, January 20, 2002, C1, C8.

7. "Lincoln Normal School," Alabama State Historical Marker, Marion, Alabama.

8. Drew Jubera, "Strong Rural Roots Shaped Proud Life," *Atlanta Journal-Constitution*, February 7, 2006, D4, D6.

9. Pierre Ruhe, "Music Student First: Singing in Church and College Led Her to Her Destiny," *Atlanta Journal-Constitution*, February 7, 2006, D6.

10. Coretta Scott King, *My Life With Martin Luther King, Jr.* (New York: Holt, Rinehart, and Winston, 1969), 34.

11. Ibid., 26.

12. Ibid., 39.

Chapter 2

JOURNEY NORTH AND BACK

When Coretta graduated from Lincoln High School in 1945, she followed her sister, Edythe, to Antioch College in Yellow Springs, Ohio. Antioch was a liberal arts college that had been founded by members of the Christian Community in 1852. Famed educator Horace Mann served as the institution's first president. The college's curriculum combined semesters of academic study with semesters of work and community involvement. Students' evaluations came as a result of writing assignments and reflective discussions on their experiences with faculty and colleagues rather than tests. The motto of Antioch was, "Be ashamed to die until you have won some victory for humanity."[1]

Edythe had learned about Antioch because the Lincoln High School chorus had visited there during a concert tour. Antioch was about to integrate, and they awarded Edythe a full scholarship for one year, making her one of the first African American students to enroll at Antioch.

CORETTA'S ANTIOCH YEARS

Going to college had been a dream of Coretta's throughout her adolescence. In an essay that she wrote in 1948 for *Opportunity: The Journal of Negro Life* (published by the National Urban League), she recalled that her inspiration to go to college came from watching her teachers in Alabama:

> These college graduates who taught me, I soon saw, were different from other people I knew. They had greater freedom of

movement: they went on trips; they visited cities; they knew more about the world. They had greater economic security. Although I know they weren't paid high salaries, they didn't seem to worry about money the way everyone else I knew did. They got more enjoyment out of life: they knew many different kinds of people; they could talk with pleasure about a lot of different subjects; they enjoyed books and music. They were even aware of the need for improving the political status of the Negro in the South (but for fear of losing their jobs, they remained silent). I concluded that the difference between them and the other people I knew—who seemed to me equally good people—lay in their educations. Because of these differences I decided that I had to go to college myself.[2]

Edythe and Coretta also wanted to go to college in the North because they thought they would experience better race relations there. In her essay for *Opportunity*, Coretta noted that she thought every Southern African American should go the North for a part of her education so that she could see "that there really are some white people working for racial equality and to be able to work with them."[3]

Coretta also received a partial scholarship to Antioch. She was one of three African American students in her class, and there were a total of six African Americans (including Edythe) in the college.

Coretta's roommates were white. They got along, as she did with other members of the faculty and student body, though she noticed that they occasionally behaved in ways that manifested unspoken, but deeply ingrained prejudices. Time at Antioch made Coretta recognize that racism was an American problem, rather than just a Southern problem. On the other hand, time at Antioch (as well as her role model teachers from Lincoln) also made Coretta understand the power of interracial coalitions in working for social change.

Coretta enrolled at Antioch near the time that World War II was coming to an end. Several male students at the college were conscientious objectors to military service, and Coretta joined a student group in support of them. This involvement foreshadowed her lifelong commitment to activism for peace.

During her junior year, Coretta dated a white Jewish man, a fellow music student, despite the expectation of her classmates that she would date the only African American male who was a student. Their relationship ended when he graduated.

Edythe and Coretta both found that being a pioneer in integrating a historically white institution was not easy. Ultimately, Edythe left Antioch and graduated from Ohio State, where there were more African American students and faculty. Coretta remained at Antioch.

STUDIES, MUSIC, AND WORK

Though Coretta had been valedictorian of her high school class in the South, she found that academically she was behind many of the other Antioch students. She had to study a great deal in order to perform well in her courses.

One area of her studies in which she thrived was music. Her mentor was Dr. Walter Anderson, the chairman of the music department. He was also Antioch's lone African American faculty member, and he coached Coretta for her first public concert, which took place in 1948. During her time at Antioch, Coretta also sang in the choir at Second Baptist Church in Springfield, Ohio.

During another concert at Antioch, Paul Robeson, the well-known baritone, complimented Coretta's voice. One of the first African American actors to portray serious roles in the theater, Robeson had become famous during the 1920s and 1930s for stage roles such as Othello and for his performances in musicals such as *Showboat* (in which he sang "Old Man River"). In addition, he was active nationally and internationally in social and political causes such as the antilynching movement. "More than any other performer of his time, he believed that the famous have a responsibility to fight for justice and peace."[4] During the 1940s, Senator Joseph McCarthy and the House Un-American Activities Committee investigated Robeson's travels and statements, suspecting him of promoting communism. In 1950, these investigations led the U.S. government to revoke Robeson's passport, which ended his international travel. Because there is no evidence to indicate the date of Robeson's appearance at Antioch, it is not possible to know whether or not his passport had yet been revoked when he visited the college. Nonetheless, Paul Robeson served as another role model for Coretta, as his life involved music and work for social justice. In addition, Robeson suffered as a result of the U.S. government's fears of communism during the Cold War. Similar concerns would lead the FBI to investigate and spy on Coretta and Martin during their work in the civil rights movement.

While Coretta had a great deal of work experience from the family farm in Alabama, her work and community service assignments at Antioch also offered a variety of new opportunities. During the school term, she worked as a waitress in the student dining hall. Another summer she was a counselor at an arts and music camp for students from a settlement house in the Yellow Springs area. For a semester, she worked at the Friendly Inn

Settlement House, located in the slums of Cleveland. This exposed her to urban poverty, and in her autobiography she reflected that she grew up a lot through this experience. She also worked in the science and music libraries at Antioch, at day care centers on campus and in Yellow Springs, and at the Riverside Branch of the New York Public Library.

One summer she returned to Alabama to work for her father who had opened a general store. She set up his bookkeeping system and also waited on customers. This experience reminded her of the great internal strengths that her parents held, as they strove to always be the best they could be and to make things better for their children.

The combination of these experiences prepared her for what was her final struggle at Antioch. Coretta was the first African American to major in elementary education. As a senior, she needed to practice teach in a public school. The Yellow Springs public schools did not have any African American faculty members, so her advisers told her that she would need to practice teach in another community, Xenia, in a segregated school. Coretta refused, noting that she had left the South to avoid segregation. She appealed to the president of Antioch to intervene on her behalf with the Yellow Springs authorities, but he declined. Coretta completed her practice teaching at the laboratory school on the Antioch campus, which was integrated. The situation left her disillusioned, yet it also motivated Coretta to join the student National Association for the Advancement of Colored People (NAACP) chapter, as well as the Race Relations Committee and the Civil Liberties Committee. It also was an occasion in which Coretta showed independence and determination to find a way to cope with the situation without compromising her principles.

Coretta graduated from Antioch in 1951. Thanks to the encouragement of Dr. Anderson and Mrs. Jesse Treichler (another music faculty member), she determined that she would continue her musical training. She applied to several graduate schools of music, including Juilliard and the New England Conservatory (NEC). Because she had not enjoyed living in New York during her college work experience there, she aimed to go to NEC, which was in Boston.

GRADUATE SCHOOL

The New England Conservatory accepted Coretta, and she also obtained a fellowship from the Jessie Smith Noyes Foundation, which covered her tuition. She arrived in Boston and began to seek ways to pay for her room and board. Determined not to ask her parents for money, she had to "make do" without much spending money, and she subsisted on simple meals that she could make at home, such as peanut butter sandwiches, rather than going out to eat. She connected with a white woman who was a patron of Antioch, who let her rent a room in exchange for housework. She also made friends with a network of African American women who provided support by helping her find jobs and make ends meet. These contacts came through the National Urban League, an organization chartered in 1910 to assist Southern African Americans who had migrated to the north. Through organizations such as the Urban League, Coretta saw how the African American community and its efforts for mutual aid could extend beyond a single town or region.

Coretta's course of study at the Conservatory was very challenging, even for a person who had made straight As at Antioch. In her first year, she took voice lessons as well as courses in Italian and French diction, sight-singing, harmony, music history, choir-conducting, counter-point, piano, and drama. She struggled with the piano and in 1953 was put on academic probation for lack of proficiency with it. However, her final report card noted that she had made "excellent progress" on the piano through additional practicing. Once she determined that a career as a concert singer was unlikely, she switched her major from vocal performance to music education, which meant that she had to take courses in multiple instruments.[5]

Still, singing remained her favorite part of musical study. Florence Dunn, who played piano for Coretta during graduate school, recalled "Singing put her up there, in front of an audience, preparing her to be an actor with her voice. You have to have a certain manner to be a singer, and she had it. She had wonderful presence."[6]

In her second semester, she received a grant from the State of Alabama that covered her tuition. Coretta was one of many African American students who were supported by Southern states in attending leading Northern graduate schools because the governments in their home states would not agree to integrate or to provide graduate school options for African Americans.

COURTSHIP WITH MARTIN LUTHER KING, JR.

During her second semester at NEC, in 1952, Coretta met Martin Luther King, Jr. A mutual friend, Mary Powell, gave Coretta's phone number to Martin. He called her, introduced himself, and they chatted about their studies and backgrounds. Martin flirted with her and implied that he was desperate for her to agree to date him: "You know every Napoleon has his Waterloo. I'm like Napoleon. I'm at my Waterloo, and I'm on my knees."[7]

They met the next day to have lunch. Coretta's first thoughts were that he was short and unimposing. But as he talked, she became impressed with his words and ideas. Their first conversation included discussion about the problems of racial and economic injustice as well as the need for peace in the world. Over lunch, Martin told Coretta that her character, intelligence, personality, and beauty made her a worthy potential wife. Though she reminded him that he did not know her yet, he asked Coretta to see him again, and this began a rapid courtship.

Coretta and Martin shared an interest in religion and philosophy, as well as a commitment to social justice. Around the time of her enrollment at NEC, Coretta had decided that she wanted to move away from the fundamentalist faith of her upbringing. She was in the process of reading about the Quakers and Unitarianism. Another possibility that she was considering was that she would not join a church at all and would instead practice her spiritual beliefs outside the context of organized religion.

The fact that Martin Luther King, Jr., was already a minister when they met could have been a challenge, given the status of Coretta's faith journey at the time. However, as he described what he had studied at Crozer Seminary and the research that he was pursuing at Boston University, Coretta was interested. They discussed Kant, Hegel, Nietzsche, and Thoreau as well as modern theologians such as Niebuhr and Rauschenbusch. Martin had begun to be very interested in Gandhi and his ideas of nonviolence. He took Coretta to hear him preach at the Twelfth Street Baptist Church in Roxbury, Massachusetts, and she was very impressed. She was also pleased that he indicated he didn't believe that she would have to be rebaptized by immersion in order to become a part of the Baptist faith of his roots.

Another common interest of Coretta's and Martin's was music. On a date he took her to Boston's Symphony Hall to hear pianist Arthur Rubinstein. Coretta recalled, "As Martin made comments on the various selections I thought at first that he wanted to impress me that he knew about music, too. But he was genuinely pleased to be able to take me to this concert which I could not have otherwise afforded; he was so happy in my pleasure that I stopped being watchful. We shared the concert together and enjoyed it very much."[8]

MEETING THE PARENTS

Coretta and Martin became closer during 1952. However, a hurdle to their relationship was that Martin's parents (and in particular his father) had selected another woman, the daughter of an established Atlanta family, as their ideal daughter-in-law. Both Mary Powell and Martin told Coretta about the other girlfriend, although Martin insisted that he would make up his own mind.

Coretta visited Atlanta and met the Kings during summer 1952. The Kings were middle class, urban, and Baptist, quite different from the working-class, rural, Methodist background that she had come from in Alabama. But one thing that both families shared in common was pride in their children, as well as the strong conviction that their children should achieve in learning and work.

In addition, Martin's father, who was called "Daddy King," also had rural roots, whether he wanted to admit it or not. He was the son of share-croppers from Henry County, Georgia. The eldest of nine children, he moved to Atlanta as a teenager, inspired by a minister who spoke out against segregation. Daddy King was licensed to preach and began his career, despite having little formal education. His sister was also in Atlanta, boarding in the home of A. D. Williams, the pastor of Ebenezer Baptist Church. When he came to visit his sister, he also began to court the Rev. Williams' daughter, Alberta. They were soon married and established their family, although they continued to live in the Williams' home. Daddy King also gained entrance to the Morehouse College Pastors' Training Program through the appeal of John Hope, the president of Atlanta University. When A. D. Williams died, Daddy King followed him as the pastor of Ebenezer.

By the age of 15, Martin had already become the assistant pastor to his father. This was another expectation about which Martin had talked to Coretta. As the wife of a minister of a thriving Baptist church, she would be expected to maintain an attractive personal appearance and to be dedicated to the work of the church. While he definitely wanted a wife that he could talk to about intellectual matters, he also required a wife who would respect and work with all of the church members, educated or not. Coretta's dreams of being a concert musician who traveled and lived the life of excitement would have to be sacrificed once she committed to marry him.

Daddy King visited Martin in Boston during November 1952. When he saw how much time Coretta was spending with his son, he began to talk more about the other woman in Atlanta. Martin did not argue with his father, but he asserted to friends (and ultimately to his mother) that he would be marrying Coretta. Eventually Daddy King came to the realization that this would occur, and Martin and Coretta became engaged after his father's visit. They announced their engagement in the *Atlanta Daily World* around Easter 1953, and they were married on June 18, 1953.

A WEDDING IN ALABAMA WITH AN ATLANTA PREACHER

The ceremony was at Coretta's parents' home in Alabama, with Daddy King as minister. All of the King family came from Atlanta, accompanied by several deacons and other family friends, making the Scott–King wedding one of the largest in the African American community ever to be held in rural Perry County. Coretta wore a pastel, waltz-length gown that she had purchased in Boston. She cooked the dinner that the family shared to get acquainted prior to the ceremony. She, Edythe, and Martin's sister, Christine, picked vines and flowers to decorate the wedding arch.

At Coretta's request Daddy King omitted the vow that she would "obey" her husband. This request to change the vows was not common for brides of this time period. Daddy King did not agree with the request, but he complied as he realized that both his son and Coretta had ideas of their own.

Because there were not hotels available for African Americans in the area, the newlyweds spent their wedding night in Marion at the home of Robert E. Tubbs, an undertaker. Martin later teased his wife that their marriage had begun in a funeral home. Nevertheless, African American–owned funeral homes were vital community institutions under segregation because they owned equipment (such as folding chairs, tents, and cars) that could be used for multiple purposes. They also were some of the first places in the community to have telephones.

The newlyweds traveled straight to Atlanta, where the Kings gave them a reception. Because Coretta didn't have to cook or set up for this event, she noted that she enjoyed it more than the wedding ceremony.

BECOMING A BAPTIST AND BEGINNING MARRIED LIFE

The following Sunday, Coretta joined Ebenezer Baptist Church. Daddy King baptized her by immersion, according to the Baptist practice. The family had discussed options, and Coretta had determined that she did not object any more, as going through this process would probably put her in better standing as a Baptist minister's wife.

The family stayed in Atlanta over the summer, and Coretta worked as a clerk for the Atlanta Citizens Trust Company bank, of which Daddy King was a director. Following the tradition that Daddy King had begun with the Rev. Williams, Martin and Coretta lived with the Kings in their home on "Bishop's Row" around the corner from Ebenezer Baptist Church.

In September 1953, Coretta and Martin returned to Boston. Coretta took a heavy load of courses to finish her degree at the Conservatory, focusing on music education with a major in voice and a minor in violin. She also had to be familiar with all of the different families of instruments (percussion, strings, woodwinds, and brass) so that she could teach them. This led to a lot of practice time, so Martin helped out with the house cleaning and cooking. The newlyweds were very busy with their school obligations, yet they had more time to get to know each other and to build life as a couple within this brief period than they would have for the rest of their married life.

During her last semester, Coretta practice taught at a high school and two elementary schools. She was a trailblazer in that she was the first African America to practice teach at these schools where the students were all white. The experience was much more positive than the experience that she had in Ohio. Her pupils accepted her and learned well, and her supervisor complimented her on the success of her efforts.

Coretta and Martin's social life in Boston, on the other hand, remained segregated. While a few whites would occasionally visit the meetings of the Friday night Philosophy Club that they attended, on the whole, African American students lived in different neighborhoods from white ones.

RETURN TO THE SOUTH

By winter 1954, Coretta had graduated, and Martin had almost completed his course work. He had begun to do research and writing toward his dissertation. While he occasionally talked about the possibility of pursuing an academic post, his main efforts went toward identifying a church where he would be the pastor. Several churches invited him to give trial sermons.

Though Coretta was reluctant to return to the South, such was the destiny that Martin heard calling him. Through the intercession of T. M. Alexander, a friend of the King family's from Atlanta, Martin was invited to preach at Dexter Avenue Baptist Church in Montgomery, Alabama. He would be the replacement for Dr. Vernon Johns, another scholar-preacher who had urged the members of his congregation to work for social justice.

Dexter offered Martin a beginning salary of $4,200 a year, which made him the highest-paid African American minister in Montgomery. He assumed the pastorate in May 1954, the same month that the Supreme Court handed down the *Brown v. the Board of Education* decision, which stated that the segregation of schools by race was a violation of the Equal Protection Clause of the Fourteenth Amendment to the Constitution.

Another historic event in 1954, which would later have impact on the life and work of Martin and Coretta, was the surrender of the French Command at Dien Bien Phu in Vietnam.[9] This end of colonialism in the region led to the establishment of two states: North Vietnam, which was allied with communists, and South Vietnam, which was allied with the United States. Plans were put in place for there to be an election in a year to unify the country. However, out of concern about what the outcome of the election would be, the United States discouraged it from going forward as planned. The United States also sent in military advisors to support the government in the South, which was under the leadership of General Ngo Dinh Diem, as they were concerned about the spread of communism in the area.

Coretta spent part of the summer of 1954 visiting her parents in Alabama. Martin continued to work on his dissertation and traveled often between Boston, Atlanta, and Montgomery.

NOTES

1. Antioch College Web site, http://www.antioch.edu.

2. Coretta Scott, "Why I Came to College," *Opportunity: The Journal of Negro Life* xxvi:2 (April/June 1948), reprinted at www.antioch-college.edu/news/csk/college1.html.

3. Ibid.

4. "Feature Essay: Paul Robeson: American Masters," http://www.pbs.org/wnet/americanmasters/database/robeson_p.html.

5. Pierre Ruhe, "Music Student First: Singing in Church and College Led Her to Her Destiny," *Atlanta Journal-Constitution*, February 7, 2006, D6.

6. Ibid.

7. Coretta Scott King, *My Life With Martin Luther King, Jr.* (New York: Holt, Rinehart, Winston, 1969), 54.

8. Ruhe, "Music Student First."

9. Taylor Branch, *Parting the Waters: America in the King Years, 1954–1963* (New York: Touchstone, 1988), 112–113.

Chapter 3

BEGINNINGS: FAMILY, WORK, MOVEMENT

Coretta made her first visit to Dexter Avenue Baptist Church in July 1954, and she and Martin took up residence at the parsonage at 309 S. Jackson Street in September.

DEXTER AVENUE BAPTIST CHURCH

Dexter Avenue Baptist Church sat in the middle of Montgomery, across the street from the state Supreme Court Building and diagonally across a square from the State Capitol. Shortly after the Civil War, a group of African Americans broke away from the First Baptist Church to establish Dexter, and they purchased the lot for the church in 1879. At the time there were other African American–owned properties in downtown Montgomery, but over the years, as Alabama established its Jim Crow laws, the African Americans were forced out, leaving Dexter as a last reminder to African Americans of former days.

Dexter's sanctuary held 400 worshippers, a few more than half of the size of the group that would fit into Ebenezer Baptist, Martin's home church, but several times the size of Mt. Tabor AME-Zion, Coretta's home church. Most of the members were professors at Alabama State University who lived in other parts of town and had cars to drive to church. The congregants were educated and professional, and they put great value on ministers' ideas and oratory.

The congregation, and in particular the deacons, had a reputation for controlling the direction at the church. Martin quickly set out to change this scenario and to assert his leadership. He presented an annual plan to his congregation early in his tenure. He adopted ideas that his father had used at Ebenezer, such as setting up monthly "birthday clubs," which would make special contributions to the church in honor of their months of birth.[1]

He also invited Coretta to address the congregation as part of his first service. She told them that she was pleased to be in Montgomery and their minister's wife, and she invited their prayers, as she was new at being a minister's wife. The members welcomed her and also set to getting her involved in church activities, from the women's society to the choir.

Coretta remembered that many members commented how young she appeared. She reminded them her husband had a young wife because he was a young man. In fact, Martin was two years younger than Coretta, but his confidence and eloquence quickly made him grow in stature in the eyes of his congregation.

RACE RELATIONS IN MONTGOMERY

Another thing that Martin promoted during his first year was for members to be involved with the local chapter of the NAACP. Formed in 1909 by an interracial group, the NAACP worked for the repeal of Jim Crow statutes and the expansion of voting rights for African Americans. They also spoke out against negative portrayals of African Americans in literature and film, most notably in a campaign against D. W. Griffith's racist film *The Birth of a Nation* (1915). In the 1930s, the NAACP formed a unit that mounted legal challenges to segregation in educational institutions, an effort that culminated in their role as plaintiffs' attorneys in *Brown v. the Board of Education*.

Though the NAACP had a long history of diverse accomplishments, it (and any other group that publicly sought to challenge the status quo) was extremely controversial in Jim Crow Alabama. Ultimately, the State of Alabama banned the NAACP during the Montgomery Bus Boycott for its refusal to release a list of members. The NAACP refused to release its membership list because it knew that doing so would lead to immediate retaliation and firings of members. By the time the NAACP sued and won the right to protect the privacy of its membership list, other organizations such as the Montgomery Improvement Association (MIA) had formed to advocate for civil rights in Alabama.

Dexter Avenue Baptist sponsored and hosted mass meetings about issues of community concern. Martin also strongly suggested that Dexter members should be registered voters, a situation that made the congregation extra special because less than 5 percent of eligible African Americans were registered to vote in Alabama.[2]

PASTORAL FAMILY LIFE

Because she had professional training, Coretta quickly became a big asset to the Dexter music program. She sang solos and helped plan the music for worship. To provide opportunities to area musicians, she also organized cultural programs for the community. As a part of a week of services focused on youth, she planned a talent show featuring local young people.

Thus, the first 15 months in Montgomery were very busy for Coretta and Martin. Both of them established themselves as parts of the community. Martin completed his dissertation and returned to Boston to defend; Coretta retyped it—all 350 pages. She also served as his secretary in Montgomery. They would discuss his sermon ideas as he was in the process of preparing them, and during church services, she would listen closely in order to give a critique.

The members of Dexter Avenue Baptist Church took pride that their new pastoral family were newlyweds. They redecorated the parsonage and sought to provide for what the family would need.

The church used the parsonage as a place for social gatherings and small group meetings. The house's layout showed this emphasis on space that could be shared with the church community. It had a den, living room, dining room, kitchen, bathroom, and only one bedroom. There was a large front porch with a swing. The telephone was in the hall, which ran down the middle of the home. Later, the church members added an office/study for Martin, in which a second telephone line was installed.[3]

The Kings made friends with another Baptist pastoral couple, Ralph and Juanita Abernathy. Ralph pastored First Baptist Church, which was the church that Dexter emerged out of. First Baptists' members were less affluent, and the worship style was more emotional and less academic. Yet, any rivalry between the churches did not impact on the bond between the couples.

On November 17, 1955, Coretta's life changed, as she became a mother for the first time. Yolanda Denise was born in St. Jude's Hospital, a segregated Catholic facility. Assuming that he and Coretta would have a son, Martin had already planned to name the baby Martin Luther King III. When Yolanda was born, he did not have a girl's name picked out, so Coretta chose Yolanda's name. Martin teased her that about her choice and suggested that Yolanda was hard to pronounce. However, they settled on a nickname, "Yoki," which Yolanda's friends and family called her for the entirety of her life.

ROSA PARKS AND THE
MONTGOMERY BUS BOYCOTT

Coretta only had a short time to adjust to motherhood and family life before an event happened that affected her family greatly. On Thursday, December 1, 1955, Rosa Parks was arrested after refusing to give up her seat on a bus to a white man. Rosa Parks was a seamstress at the Montgomery Fair department store. She was also a highly respected member of NAACP who had attended civil rights training sessions at the Highlander Folk School. E. D. Nixon, a leader in the local Brotherhood of Sleeping Car Porters, bailed Mrs. Parks out of jail, accompanied by white attorney Clifford Durr. At home with the Parks family, Nixon suggested that they organize a boycott of the Montgomery bus system in response to this injustice. On December 2, Nixon contacted Martin to enlist his involvement. Via another channel, Jo Ann Robinson, a faculty member at Alabama State, a leader in the Women's Political Caucus, and a member of Dexter Avenue Baptist, created and distributed thousands of fliers calling for the community to boycott the buses and to attend a mass meeting the following Monday night at Holt Street Baptist Church, Rosa Parks' church. On Monday morning, Coretta was the first to see that the buses passing along Jackson Street were almost empty—a sign that the African American community had embraced the effort. She and Martin rejoiced together before he set out with Ralph Abernathy to see how the effort was going around the city.

At the meeting on Monday night, the attendees formed the MIA to guide their boycott. They selected Martin to be the president. Since Coretta was unable to attend the mass meeting, she arranged for Martin's speech to be recorded, beginning a practice that would later help the King Family preserve an archive of his words and writings.[4]

Coretta did not attend these mass meetings because she was at home taking care of Yolanda. When Martin shared the news that he would be the president of the MIA, he told Coretta that he had been drafted into the role. Coretta did not protest and supported him in his work.[5]

The parsonage quickly became one of the command centers for MIA activities. The phone rang constantly, both with calls from supporters and movement participants and with threats from white supremacists. Martin was arrested, supposedly for speeding, on January 26. This was the first of many times during their married life that Coretta had to endure her husband being locked up on trumped up charges. Fortunately, he was released soon after, on his own recognizance, after the arrival of Ralph Abernathy on the scene.

The Dexter membership and other community members rallied around the Kings. They were particularly concerned about Coretta staying at home alone. While she said that she was comfortable staying alone and unafraid, they began to organize for women to visit with her while Martin was away at mass meetings.

On January 30, 1956, the King parsonage was bombed. Coretta was at home with Mary Lucy Williams, the wife of a Dexter deacon. She heard a "thump" on the porch and suggested that she and Mary move to the rear of the house. The dynamite exploded, broke glass at the front of the home, and sent smoke throughout it. It left a dent in the concrete of the porch, but it did not cause severe structural damage. Because they had moved into the back bedroom, Coretta, Mary, and Yolanda were not hurt.

Neighbors quickly gathered. Coretta called Ralph Abernathy's church, where Martin was speaking that night. A female member answered the phone. She first passed a message to Ralph, who later informed Martin of the news. Martin cut short the mass meeting and rushed home.

He found a large crowd gathered in his yard. The mayor of Montgomery was there as was the police commissioner. His first priority was to check on Coretta and Yolanda, and once he determined that they were all right, he realized that he needed to encourage the crowd to move on. There was tension in the air, particularly among young men.

Martin asked Coretta to get dressed—she had been in her robe at the time of the bombing. He then brought her out onto the porch to demonstrate that she was unharmed and that she was calm throughout the trial. Then he urged the crowd to remain calm, urging them to respond to the bombing with nonviolence. He reminded the crowd of Jesus' caution that, "he who lives by the sword, dies by the sword," as well as of the commandment to Jesus' followers to love their enemies.

Martin's sermon, and Coretta's calm reaction to the incident, prevented what could have been an explosion of violence in Montgomery. In response, the mayor and police commissioner promised additional protection of the King home, as well as a full investigation and effort to locate the perpetrators, which included a $5,000 reward. The bombers were never identified or located, but the Dexter community members organized additional security for the parsonage, including spotlights and evening guards. There were other bombings in Montgomery, including incidents at the homes of E. D. Nixon and Ralph Abernathy. Dynamite was tossed at the King parsonage a second time, but this time it was discovered prior to explosion.

Martin and Coretta both faced pressure from their respective parents to leave Montgomery and to cease involvement in the movement. Daddy King was particularly insistent that Martin should return to Atlanta. After a tense discussion, during which Martin reiterated his desire to stay in Montgomery, Martin thanked Coretta and reminded her of how important her support had been during their difficulties. While Martin and Coretta were in Atlanta on a visit during the boycott, Daddy King enlisted the support of Dr. Benjamin Mays to help with his persuasion. Martin continued to insist that his work was in Montgomery, and Coretta assured Martin that she would continue to stand by him: "Whatever you decide to do, I will always be with you."[6]

So they returned to Montgomery to continue their work during the boycott. Martin was arrested a second time in March 1956 for organizing a boycott, which was against the laws of Alabama. He was found guilty and sentenced to pay a $500 fine or to serve over a year of hard labor. Martin's lawyers appealed and filed a suit in federal court questioning the constitutionality of segregation on buses. The federal court ruled in the favor of the MIA. Immediately, the city of Montgomery appealed to the U.S. Supreme Court, who upheld the ruling of the federal court in November 1956 via *Browder v. Gayle*. Coretta was in the courtroom at the time this decision was announced.

Montgomery's buses integrated on December 21, 1956. For two days there were no incidents. Early in the morning of December 23, someone shot bullets through the front door of the Kings' home. The Kings were inside, but no one was injured. The next day King stated to the Dexter congregation, "It may be that some of us have to die." At a mass meeting he sent a message to the unidentified attackers: "I would like to tell whoever did it that it won't do any good to kill me."[7] While Coretta recognized the theological truth behind these words, as a young mother and wife, they terrified her. Martin also announced that the MIA's work was not complete via the integration of buses and that the next effort would be toward the integration of schools.

A FAMOUS HUSBAND AND
A WIFE WHO HELPS OUT

Thanks to the success of the Montgomery Bus Boycott and Martin's leadership, the Kings gained additional visibility. *Jet* magazine put Martin and Coretta on their cover, proclaiming him "Alabama's Modern Moses."

Reporters came from across the United States and around the world. Intellectuals, activists, and political workers also came to meet the Kings and to get involved in the boycott. Bayard Rustin, who would eventually work closely with Martin over the rest of his life, arrived bearing a note of introduction from one of Coretta's former teachers from Lincoln High School in Marion.

As the MIA's mission grew, the need increased for fundraising and organizational management. In December 1956, Ella Baker, Stanley Levison, and Bayard Rustin organized a fundraiser for the MIA in New York City. Baker was a veteran member of the NAACP who had organized youth chapters across the South prior to moving to New York. She later became executive director of the Southern Christian Leadership Conference (SCLC). Levison was an attorney and veteran fundraiser; this encounter began a lifelong association between him and the Kings. The concert date marked the first anniversary of Rosa Parks' arrest. Duke Ellington and Harry Belafonte performed. Coretta organized a presentation using story and music to provide an account of the Montgomery Bus Boycott. She drew on a model of a program that she had performed during her days as a student at Lincoln High School. She also continued to use this model for the Freedom Concerts that would come later in her life.

Coretta's musical gifts also came in handy in other contexts. She sang for the Omega Psi Phi fraternity national conclave in Baltimore in 1956, where Martin received an award. At this meeting, the Kings met Harris Wofford, the first white man to graduate from Howard University's Law School and another student of Gandhi's nonviolent philosophy. Wofford later became a key contact between the Kings and John and Robert Kennedy.

In January 1957, Martin's work entered a new phase. A group of pastors gathered in Atlanta to discuss forming a regional organization to work for civil rights, along the model of the MIA. Prior to the meeting, Martin and Ralph Abernathy had to leave suddenly, after Juanita called and reported that their home had been bombed, as well as four churches and another home. Coretta filled in for Martin, opening the meeting, explaining his absence, and presenting the agenda. She presided until he could return to Atlanta the following day. The group determined that a second, larger meeting would be held in New Orleans in February, and it was there that the SCLC was established.

In March 1957, the Kings traveled to Africa to witness the establishment of Ghana as the first African nation to emerge from colonialism. Dexter Baptist provided them a bonus to support the trip, along with another contribution from the MIA. The Kings were part of a delegation that included other African American dignitaries, such as Ralph Bunche, Adam Clayton Powell, A. Philip Randolph, Roy Wilkins, and Lester Granger. In addition, they met Vice President Richard Nixon, who was representing the U.S. government. Nixon invited Martin to Washington for a private briefing on civil rights. The trip made Martin see connections between his work and efforts to relieve oppression around the world. While there was much work to be done back home, both he and Coretta maintained an interest in international work throughout the rest of their lives.

Coretta and Martin returned via Rome, Geneva, Paris, and London. Martin used the trip as the subject matter for a sermon at Dexter upon their return in order to thank the congregation for supporting the voyage.

The year 1957 also saw Martin receive the Spingarn Medal from the NAACP; his first honorary doctorate from Morehouse; and additional cover stories in *Jet* magazine. He was highly in demand as a speaker, and he traveled greatly. He also began to write a monthly column in *Ebony*, "Advice for Living."

Meanwhile, Coretta was expecting their second child. When she gave birth to Martin Luther King III on October 23, 1957, Martin was conducting the annual business meeting of Dexter Avenue Baptist Church. A courier delivered the message to the happy father, who only briefly interrupted the meeting for a celebration. Later, a church member called the hospital to report to Coretta that Dr. King was detained. Several of the church women gathered in the hall and grumbled, considering it inappropriate that he didn't cut the meeting shorter and go to the hospital.[8]

In the summer of 1958, the Kings took a two-week vacation to Mexico. This was one of the first times in a long period in which they had been able to travel without him having appointments or speaking engagements. Coretta noted that Mexico presented a dilemma to them—it was a beautiful country, but there was such a stark contrast between the living conditions of the rich, who had every luxury, and the poor, who lived in slums in utter destitution.

Tensions about money and material status would remain a factor throughout Martin and Coretta's life together. Martin occasionally expressed a desire to Coretta not to own things—considering material things unimportant and distractions away from the spiritual life. On the other hand, from his youth he was accustomed to a middle-class lifestyle, which included certain comforts. He accepted his position as the pastor at Dexter with the highest salary for a minister in Montgomery, and he had also been willing to accept bonuses from the church to support ventures such as the trip to Ghana. In addition, he was a stylish dresser, and even back to the days of his dating Coretta, he had encouraged her to take pride in herself and to present a polished image, as was fitting the wife of a minister. Coretta, who had actually grown up poor, found a way to reconcile Martin's various statements by not taking any one of them too seriously. She did not seek material things to excess, but she also would not allow her young family to be subjected to unnecessary hardships.

Some of the tension about material status came out of the fact that Martin was studying Gandhi during this period. Prominent Indians came to Montgomery to meet with him and exchange ideas on nonviolence. The chairman of the Gandhi Memorial Trust suggested to Martin that he must "prepare not just to talk about suffering but to endure physical sacrifice himself."[9]

Another tension that grew during this period, and that also continued, was between Martin's commitment to the family on the one hand and to the movement and larger society on the other. Coretta recalled that he once stated, "You know, a man who dedicates himself to a cause doesn't need a family." Yet, because Coretta was confident of Martin's love for her and for the children, she did not take those words seriously. She recognized that he felt a strong call to serve his people and that he was resisting a pull to devote himself completely to that call. Owing to his upbringing and other influences on his life, he also needed to have a family, and, in fact, having a family made him more identifiable to those he was seeking to lead.

In September 1958, Martin was arrested again, while he waited to speak to his attorney during a trial involving Ralph Abernathy. Coretta was also at the scene of this arrest, but she managed to avoid arrest through remaining silent. Martin was sentenced to 14 days in jail or a $14 fine. He stated that he would go to jail and serve the sentence. However, the police commissioner paid his fine in order to prevent giving Martin a platform to point out the injustice of his arrest.

Martin did suffer physically later that month. During a book signing in New York City, Izola Ware Curry, a mentally unstable woman, stabbed him in the chest with a letter opener. She reported that she had been tracking Martin for a long period of time. Coretta found out about this incident through a telephone call from a New York pastor. She headed for New York, and Martin's sister, Christine, joined her in Atlanta. She arrived for Martin's recovery, after he had undergone surgery that involved the removal of two ribs and part of his breastbone. The weapon had grazed his aorta, and doctors noted that this had been a very close call for him. Still, as he reflected on the event with Coretta, he did not hold a grudge against his attacker because he knew she was disturbed. He recovered in New York, and Coretta stayed with him for three weeks. Because of Martin's injury, Coretta substituted for him at the October 1958 Youth March and Rally for Desegregation, led by Jackie Robinson and Harry Belafonte.[10]

In February 1959, the Kings traveled to India so that Martin could continue his study of nonviolence. The trip involved several episodes that defied his claims to wanting to live a simple life. First, the Kings knew that they would be meeting with Prime Minister Nehru and other important officials, which required them to bring formal clothes. They overloaded their suitcases and faced an excess baggage fee. They also changed travel plans mid-trip, to include a stopover in Paris to meet Richard Wright, author of *Native Son*. That change caused them to miss a flight connection, which made them late for their expected arrival. There were 500 Indian citizens gathered at the airport for an arrival ceremony, but the Kings did not arrive. Their hosts had to organize a separate, smaller greeting party to meet them when they arrived the following evening.

The Kings attended a dinner party with Prime Minister Nehru. They also met Lady Mountbatten of England. Martin and Nehru discussed the comparison of the African American freedom struggle and that of the Indian Independence movement. Coretta listened to their four-hour conversation. Reflecting back on it, she stated that she probably would have wanted to discuss some other issues, especially as she learned more about the status of women in India. During the trip, she joined the Women's International League for Peace and Freedom.

The rest of the trip included visits to sites significant to the life of Gandhi. They laid a wreath at his tomb. They also saw the site of the salt march. The Kings perceived a contradiction between the words and actions of their Indian hosts. The Indians spoke about the importance of living simply, yet they surrounded themselves with material comforts.

After the trip, Martin began to emphasize even more his desire to live simply. He felt the United States, like India, was subject to the corruption of material things. When unsolicited donations came in, Martin insisted that they be devoted to the movement rather than to him personally. While Coretta served as a sounding board for Martin's ideas and beliefs, she and the children also helped him remain grounded, as he recognized that it would be wrong to force them to live without a modest level of material comforts.

Yet, Coretta also saw the masses of African American people gaining a love for Martin that bordered on worship. Just as the Indians lived luxuriously to make up for their years of suffering, the Americans thought that nothing was too good for Martin. Reflecting back, Coretta noted that "they thought of him as the outstanding person of the race in the world. He was, to many of them, the President of the Negroes."[11] This status continued for the Kings and affected the ways in which the public treated Coretta and the children after Martin's death.

NOTES

1. Taylor Branch, *Parting the Waters: America in the King Years, 1954–1963* (New York: Touchstone, 1988), 115.

2. Ibid., 116.

3. Dexter Parsonage Museum, Montgomery, Alabama.

4. "King Room Exhibit," Freedom Hall, Martin Luther King, Jr. Center for Nonviolent Social Change, Atlanta, Georgia.

5. Branch, *Parting,* 137.

6. Ibid., 135.

7. David Garrow, *Bearing the Cross: Martin Luther King, Jr. and the Southern Christian Leadership Conference* (New York: Harper Collins, 1986), 83.

8. Branch, *Parting,* 229.

9. Ibid. 237.

10. "King Room Exhibit," Freedom Hall.

11. Coretta Scott King, *My Life With Martin Luther King, Jr.* (New York: Holt, Rinehart, Winston, 1969), 180.

Chapter 4

PUTTING DOWN ROOTS IN ATLANTA

Martin resigned as pastor of Dexter Avenue Baptist Church in November 1959 in order to return to Atlanta, where he became copastor with Daddy King of Ebenezer Baptist Church. This job allowed him to devote additional time to the work of the SCLC, which involved much speaking, organizing, and fundraising. Atlanta seemed the natural location because it was becoming a major transportation hub.

BACK TO ATLANTA

As Coretta knew, Atlanta was Martin's home town, and he had grown up in the heart of the African American middle-class social establishment. Though Coretta's roots were in a completely different type of context, by this point, she had been a minister's wife in a city for long enough to understand the roles that she should play. Coretta recognized that Ebenezer was an important church in the Atlanta African American community and that she would be the minister's wife, although she would also share the limelight with her mother-in-law (who also had the distinguishing characteristic of being the daughter of another revered pastor).

As Coretta set up their household, she endeavored that it met the community's standards. She arranged for the cook who had worked for them in Montgomery to move to Atlanta. She also endeared herself in social circles by phoning the wife of the president of Spelman College to seek help in identifying a "suitable" student to act as babysitter and errand runner.[1]

Coretta's actions were not fully in line with Martin's expressed desire to live simply, yet he did not interfere with Coretta's handling of the household realm. However, Martin's salary as a copastor made an impact on the level of material comforts that the family could enjoy. Ebenezer provided $6,000, which put Martin's salary well below what the highest-paid ministers in Atlanta made. He also agreed to accept only $1 per year as salary from the SCLC, which allowed him to be covered by the organization's insurance but obviously did not provide funds for the family.

At Martin's insistence, the Kings' first home in Atlanta was a rental apartment on the east side. A few years later, at Coretta's insistence, they purchased a home at 234 Sunset, but it was a modest structure, and some of the others in the neighborhood were quite rundown. By contrast, Daddy King and his wife moved to the west side, which was the newer and preferred location for middle-class African Americans.

LEGAL STRUGGLES

A financial difficulty followed the Kings from Alabama. Because of his political work and notoriety, the IRS audited the Kings, and the State of Alabama accused them of owing back taxes. Sensing that the accusations grew out of racism and displeasure at his civil rights work, Martin settled and paid back taxes to the state and federal governments about the time of their move. But the following year, he learned that the State of Alabama was upping the charge, accusing him with felony tax evasion for 1956 and 1958. Through SCLC and other contacts, a group of attorneys began to work on his defense. Coretta retrieved Martin's expense diaries out of a trunk in their attic, in which he had recorded honoraria received and business expenses. These diaries became important evidence in the efforts to show that Martin had not comingled personal and organizational funds. In a rare occurrence for the era, an all-white Alabama jury acquitted him on May 28, 1960, thanks in part to the evidence that Coretta had located.

Martin's notoriety and also segregation in Georgia led the Kings to face another challenge. On May 4, 1960, a DeKalb County police officer stopped Martin and Coretta, who were driving white author Lillian Smith (Strange Fruit, 1944) back to her home after dinner. The officer issued a ticket for Martin for driving a car with an expired Alabama tag and also for failing to obtain a Georgia drivers' license since his move into the state. Again, Martin paid the fines and received a suspended sentence.

However, this encounter with the law also came back to haunt the Kings. Martin was arrested again a few months later as part of a student protest and sit-in at Rich's department store. Coretta was at home with the children, and she learned of this arrest via a telephone call from Jesse Hill, the president of the Atlanta Life Insurance, a historic, black-owned firm. The word of Martin's arrest also reached DeKalb County, and a judge suggested that this arrest could violate the terms of the suspended sentence that Martin had from the previous driving incident.

Subsequently, police transferred Martin to the DeKalb County jail, where Judge Oscar Mitchell sentenced him to four months of hard labor. Coretta became very upset at the thought of her husband being jailed in DeKalb County, which had a reputation as the home of the Ku Klux Klan. Via a phone call, Martin appealed to Coretta to remain calm and collected during these difficulties. Coretta was six months pregnant with their third child at this time and was very distraught, despite her best efforts not to appear so.

To make matters even worse, under the cover of night, the police transferred Martin to Reidsville State Prison, four hours away in South Georgia. This transfer set in motion requests for assistance from Coretta, Daddy King, and other allies. Because she was expecting, Coretta's main involvement was via making telephone calls. She reached out to Harris Wofford for help, noting that she feared for Martin's life in Reidsville. Wofford called Sargent Shriver, the brother-in-law of John Kennedy, who was a presidential candidate at the time. Shriver contacted John Kennedy and suggested that he should call Coretta. John Kennedy did call Coretta and shared his concern for her and her husband's plight. If there was anything that he could do to help, he would aim to do it. Robert Kennedy was also involved in the efforts to free Martin. He called Georgia Governor Ernest Vandiver to seek advice about contacting Judge Mitchell and asking him to release Martin. Vandiver suggested that the intermediary be George D. Stewart, the secretary of the Georgia Democratic party. Though neither Vandiver nor Stewart was a friend of the civil rights movement at the time, they agreed to present the case to Judge Mitchell, who ultimately agreed to release Martin. They also agreed that they would not broadcast news of their involvement in this situation, preferring for the public to think that Judge Mitchell had acted after a phone call from Robert Kennedy. Evidence is not clear as to the timing of that phone call—whether it was before Judge Mitchell released King or whether it was after the release, as Judge Mitchell sought to extract additional benefit from doing Kennedy this favor.[2]

When Coretta informed Daddy King about this call from John Kennedy, it led him to shift his support in the upcoming election. At a mass meeting at Ebenezer, he indicated "If I had a suitcase full of votes, I'd take them all and place them at the feet of Senator Kennedy."[3] Historians have noted that this change of endorsement and other publicity that got out about the Kennedy involvement in the King case affected the outcome of the 1960 election, in which Kennedy only won by 100,000 votes.

Coretta gave birth to their third child, Dexter Scott, on January 30, 1961. He was six weeks premature.[4] Martin was in Chicago at the time, as part of a fundraising trip for the SCLC. As the organization grew and involved itself in new efforts, such trips were an important part of Martin's duties. Increasingly they kept him away from his family, leaving Coretta to rely on other members of the King family for support.

CORETTA'S MOVEMENT WORK

Coretta also traveled and participated in some movement activities. Often her engagements were related to fundraising opportunities or to programs related to women, children, and peace. She was a delegate to the White House Conference on Children and Youth in February 1960. She also lectured and performed for the Women's Day Program at the New First Baptist Church in Charleston, West Virginia, in November 1961.

In April 1962, Coretta served as a delegate to the Women's Strike for Peace in Geneva, Switzerland.[5] This rally was in conjunction with international talks regarding a test-ban of atomic weapons. Coretta's interest in working for world peace dated back to groups she had been a part of during her college days at Antioch.

Author Alice Walker was a freshman at Spelman College in 1962. She and a group of students were also preparing to attend the World Youth Peace Festival in Helsinki that summer. Their advisor, a white peace activist from California, arranged for them to meet with Coretta, whom she saw as a role model for the students. Many years later, Walker reflected on this encounter:

> As she talked briefly to us, I sat on the sofa and stared at her, much too shy myself to speak. I was satisfied just to witness her exuberance, her brightness, her sparkle and smiles, as she talked about the peace movement, her music and all her plans. She gave us several words of encouragement about our journey, the first trip abroad for all of us, but I don't recall what they were. She did not, and we did not, mention her husband. But she was so clearly a happy woman that I couldn't help wishing I could sneak out of the living room and through the rest of the house, because I was positive he was there.[6]

BEHIND THE SCENES DURING ALBANY AND BIRMINGHAM

In 1961–62, Martin and the SCLC leadership also became involved in the Albany Movement to desegregate public facilities in Southwest Georgia. Coretta visited him in Albany and had several speaking engagements. Martin was arrested, along with Ralph Abernathy and many local citizens. Wyatt Walker, the director of the SCLC, planned a Mother's Day March, which would be led by Coretta, Juanita Abernathy, and other wives of the movement. However, local officials released King and Abernathy in an effort to minimize external attention to the situation, and the Mother's Day March did not occur. Nonetheless, out of the Albany Movement came many tactics that Martin and the SCLC would later repeat during the Birmingham Movement.

Coretta and Martin's fourth child, Bernice Albertine, was born on March 28, 1963, just before the beginning of the Birmingham desegregation campaign. Martin took Coretta to the hospital and was there during the birth. Then he immediately left for Birmingham and planning meetings. He returned to Atlanta on April 2, when Coretta came home from the hospital, and then he went back to Birmingham where protests began on April 3.

After defying a court order to cease the protest marches, Martin was arrested in Birmingham on April 12, Good Friday. He went to jail for what would become his most famous jail stay and quickly was placed in solitary confinement. Coretta, at home with a newborn, was concerned because Martin did not make the phone call home that she expected to receive. By Easter Sunday she was distraught, fearing for Martin's life. She began to make telephone calls to the White House, seeking intervention by President Kennedy. President Kennedy was out of town for the holiday, and the White House would not give her a number at which to reach him. So she reached out to diplomat Pierre Salinger, who indicated he would see what he could do. She also received a call from Harry Belafonte, who provided funds for Coretta to hire a nurse to keep the children and a secretary to handle calls so that they could travel to Birmingham and check on Martin. Attorney General Robert Kennedy also called Coretta, on behalf of the President. He indicated that he would see what he could do to help, though he also admitted that the government was facing resistance from Bull Connor and other Birmingham officials. President Kennedy called Coretta on Monday and reported that he had sent FBI agents into Birmingham who confirmed Martin's safety. He told her to expect a phone call from Martin, and one came 15 minutes later.

When Martin did call, he was being watched and listened to by Birmingham officials. He suggested that she get word to Wyatt Walker about the President's call so that he could handle the publicity via SCLC channels. Coretta had already issued a statement to the *New York Times*, so this created a predicament. In the days ahead, Birmingham officials disputed Coretta's version of the story, insisting that they had not denied Martin the right to call her and also suggesting that she was suffering depression as a new mother. Yet, the knowledge that national political figures had intervened on behalf of King and the movement strengthened their case as bearers of the moral high ground.

ONSTAGE AT THE MARCH ON WASHINGTON

Coretta and Juanita Abernathy traveled to Birmingham on April 18 to visit their husbands. During the trip, Coretta suggested to Martin that he should call for a March on Washington to highlight the need for desegregation.[7] Later in the summer, after the Birmingham Movement achieved its goal of promoting integration of the downtown businesses and parks, Martin worked with A. Philip Randolph of the Brotherhood of Sleeping Car Porters, James Farmer of Congress of Racial Equality (CORE), Roy Wilkins of the NAACP, and Whitney Young of the Urban League to do that.

The March was on August 28, 1963; 250,000 people attended and millions more watched on television. Coretta attended, although the wives of leaders were not allowed to march with their husbands or to attend the postmarch meeting at the White House with President Kennedy. These slights hurt Coretta because she recognized the role that she and other movement wives played. Wyatt Walker did find a seat for Coretta on the platform where Martin spoke his famous "I Have a Dream" speech.

Coming out of the March on Washington, it seemed that good days were ahead for those involved in the civil rights struggle. Nonetheless, President Kennedy could not raise enough support in Congress to overcome the objections of Southern senators and to pass the Civil Rights Bill.

FBI SURVEILLANCE

Martin's increase in visibility led to an unjust loss of his privacy. In October 1963, Attorney General Robert Kennedy signed an order that allowed the FBI to begin to wiretap Martin and Coretta's home, as well as the office of the SCLC. The surveillance came about at the instigation of J. Edgar Hoover, the Director of the FBI, who had been in power since

1924. Hoover commonly used wiretaps and bugs to collect information about many people whom he was investigating. From the end of WWII until the end of his career in the 1970s, much of the surveillance grew out of concern about perceived communist infiltration in the United States.

The connection to Martin that concerned the FBI was Stanley Levison, a friend and attorney that Martin met in 1956. Prior to this point, FBI informants had discovered that Levison was involved in the financial leadership of the Communist Party of the United States (CPUSA). The FBI bugged Levison, and they also closely tracked his movements. Levison ceased having involvement in the CPUSA around the same time that he met Martin, but as his friendship with Martin grew and he became more involved in Martin's business affairs, the FBI became more suspicious of Martin.

Around the time of the Birmingham campaign, Attorney General Kennedy received a memo that indicated that a close advisor of Martin's was a member of the Communist Party. They began to scrutinize other friends and associates of Martin's, and they identified several others who were suspected of communist connections. In a meeting, Attorney General Kennedy and President Kennedy suggested that Martin should cut ties to these persons, but Martin did not want to do that.

Martin enlisted Clarence Jones, another attorney and friend, to serve as intermediary between him and Levison. Suspecting that their phones were tapped, they used code terms and avoided speaking of Levison by name. This made the FBI more suspicious, and so they increased their surveillance. In addition, after some surveillance, the focus moved from Martin's alleged communist ties to other examples of behavior that they considered improper.

For the rest of Martin's life, the FBI continued to track and monitor his business dealings and personal life, including wiretaps and other surveillance. Martin, Coretta, and Martin's colleagues realized that the surveillance was underway after not much time went by, and they tempered their words and activities accordingly. However, the FBI still built a volume of material that they used to attempt to discredit Martin and to undercut his work.

SAD ROLE MODELS

During the Kennedy administration, the United States continued to maintain military advisors in Vietnam, supporting the government of General Diem and working against the growth of support for the communist government from the north. General Diem was a Catholic, and he was not sympathetic to the majority of the citizens of Vietnam, who were Buddhist. The South Vietnamese military burned temples and even attacked a crowd of Buddhists who were marking a religious holiday. These actions weakened the support for Diem. Some Buddhist monks even committed suicide in public via setting themselves on fire. Westerners learned of those acts through photographs and journalists' reports. Some Americans were horrified by these shocking acts, and they began to question the U.S. involvement in Vietnam. In November 1963, the United States responded to this concern by helping to organize a coup against General Diem. He and his brothers were also assassinated by members of the military. But out of continuing concern about communism coming into the region from the north, the United States maintained their presence of military advisors in the country.

In November 1963, President John F. Kennedy was assassinated in Dallas. In the wake of his death, popular sentiment for the civil rights bill increased. President Lyndon Baines Johnson (who succeeded Kennedy) used his knowledge of Senate parliamentary procedure and got the bill passed by both houses. He signed it into law on July 2, 1964. Martin was there, but Coretta had to remain at home with the children.

Reflecting on the assassination of President Kennedy, Coretta noted that she had paid special attention to the actions and attitude of Jacqueline Kennedy. Coretta realized the pain that she was suffering at the loss of her husband, especially as she was the mother of young children. Coretta identified with Jacqueline, even as she thought about how dangerous her own husband's work was. She stated, "It was as if watching the funeral, I was steeling myself for our own fate."[8]

In the early days of his administration, President Johnson also declared "war on poverty." He set up an Office of Economic Opportunity and antipoverty programs, ranging from Head Start to the Job Corps. He also promoted the vision of a "Great Society," in which there would be equal opportunity and improved quality of life. He provided funds to improve living conditions in rural and urban areas; he established mechanisms by which the federal government could help control air and water pollution; and he promoted education at all levels. He also advocated the continuation of civil rights gains through legislation, establishing himself as an ally of the movement.

NOTES

1. Taylor Branch, *Parting the Waters: America in the King Years, 1954–1963* (New York: Touchstone, 1988), 268.

2. Clifford M. Kuhn, "There's a Footnote to History! Memory and the History of Martin Luther King's October 1960 Arrest and its Aftermath," *The Journal of American History* 84:2 (September 1997), 576–76.

3. Coretta Scott King, *My Life With Martin Luther King, Jr.* (New York: Holt, Rinehart, Winston, 1969), 197.

4. Dexter King, *Growing Up King: An Intimate Memoir* (New York: Warner Books, 2003), 20.

5. "King Room Exhibit," Freedom Hall, Martin Luther King, Jr. Center for Nonviolent Social Change, Atlanta, Georgia.

6. Alice Walker, *In Search of Our Mother's Gardens: Womanist Prose* (San Diego: Harcourt Brace Jovanovich, 1983), 147.

7. "King Room Exhibit," Freedom Hall.

8. Scott King, *My Life With Martin Luther King, Jr.*, 245.

Chapter 5

DIFFICULT DAYS

In many ways, Birmingham and the March on Washington represented the apex of Martin's civil rights efforts. While there were still other significant challenges ahead, such as voting rights and economic justice, the days after Birmingham brought a variety of challenges to nonviolence—from white massive resistance to black power. The Kings remained under constant FBI surveillance, and once they recognized this fact, it made it difficult for them to communicate casually with friends and colleagues. On the other hand, the number of local civil rights efforts proliferated across the United States, and these led to a large volume of requests for Martin and the SCLC to participate. Martin's travel schedule was increasingly hectic as he shuttled between home, fundraisers, meetings, rallies, and speaking engagements.

Coretta remained the primary caretaker of the family and the household. Martin felt that such was the proper role for a wife, and he relied on Coretta to conform to his expectations. While Coretta accepted this role, she did complain to Martin and his associates occasionally about the frequency of his absences from home. In addition, Coretta requested that she be able to travel with Martin from time to time. When she could arrange for the children to be cared for by a relative or friend, she accompanied him on some trips, such as to give the baccalaureate address at Wesleyan University in June 1964. The family also took a vacation to the New York World's Fair in August.

In September 1964, Martin donated his personal papers to Boston University, his alma mater. This donation had been solicited by Harold DeWolf, his major professor. At the time of the donation, Martin knew that his undergraduate alma mater, Morehouse, was also interested in the collection, but Martin thought that the papers would be better cared for at Boston University, which had an established Special Collections division in their library.

In 1967, Coretta organized a meeting of supporters in Atlanta to plan for the return of the papers to their home town.[1] This was another example of Coretta taking pride in Martin's work and seeing his intellectual property as valuable. However, after the initial meeting, Martin, Coretta, and Martin's staff members all failed to inform Boston University that there was any desire for the papers to be located elsewhere.

THE FREEDOM CONCERTS

In 1964, Coretta began to travel on her own for fundraisers and other appearances. She conducted a series of Freedom Concerts, with the debut performance on November 14 in New York City. The Freedom Concerts mixed songs, poetry, and other narrations, and they told the story of the civil rights struggle. Thematic sections included "The American Dream," "The Dream Blighted," "A New Hope: Portrait of the Nonviolent Integration Movement in Montgomery," "The National Movement Deployed," "One World-One Brotherhood," "Supreme Sacrifices," "The March on Washington," and "Montgomery: the Long Road Back." The final song was "We Shall Overcome," which was becoming the anthem for the SCLC. During 1964, the concerts generated $50,000 for the SCLC and its affiliates.[2]

The Freedom Concerts continued until 1966. Venues included Trenton, Los Angeles, San Diego, San Francisco, Portland, Seattle, Pasadena, Fresno, Oakland, Phoenix, Denver, and Toronto.[3] Later, after Martin's assassination, Coretta returned to the Freedom Concert format as a fundraiser for the development of the King Center.

MARTIN'S NOBEL PRIZE

Martin's accomplishments led to an international recognition: the 1964 Nobel Peace Prize. Coretta answered a call at home from the Associated Press (AP), who broke the news. Martin was actually in the hospital recovering from exhaustion, high blood pressure, and the flu, so Coretta called him on the phone there to share the news, in hope of raising his spirits. Within two hours, Martin had verified the AP's story and arranged for a press conference at the hospital, which Coretta attended. Martin announced that he would donate the $50,000 prize to support the civil rights movement, and he made subsequent donations to the SCLC, CORE, the Student Nonviolent Coordinating Committee (SNCC), the NAACP, the National Council of Negro Women, and the American Foundation on Nonviolence.[4]

Coretta was disappointed that Martin's plans for the prize money did not include setting up a trust fund for the children. She had suggested that he set aside $10,000 for this purpose, and he declined, indicating that he had received the funds for his work with the movement and therefore the funds should go to benefit that cause.

Coretta also worried that this additional recognition would mean more travel and less opportunity for rest and family time. But as Martin stated during the press conference, "It would both be immoral and a sign of ingratitude if I did not face my moral responsibility to do what I can in this struggle."[5]

Because Martin had committed the Nobel Prize funds to the cause, he faced the challenge of raising additional funds to support the trip to Norway. A delegation of 30 family members and friends made the journey. En route they stopped in New York for a reception at the United Nations. They also stopped in London, where Martin preached at St. Paul's Cathedral. Once they arrived in Oslo, there were a series of activities that included a meeting with King Olaf.

There was some tension within the traveling party because the Abernathys (who had been close friends and coworkers in the struggle since Montgomery) were not being recognized in the same manner that the Kings were. After a conflict with the Norwegian protocol officers about limousine assignments, Juanita Abernathy fell ill and had to be hospitalized. Coretta stayed with her while the rest of the traveling group moved on to Stockholm, but eventually Coretta and Juanita rejoined the group. At a party in Stockholm, Martin and Coretta danced together, one of the few times in their lives that they did this in public. The group also traveled to Paris before returning to Atlanta.

Martin kept up appearances during the trip, but Coretta later reported that he was depressed, worried, and preoccupied. He and his SCLC colleagues had begun to plan for a voting rights campaign in Selma, Alabama, and workers who had visited the area suggested that they would face daunting challenges. Coretta recalled, "It was on his mind. He made a comment about the fact that things were going to be very difficult in Selma and that . . . those of us who were on this trip should enjoy ourselves, because somebody was going to get killed in Selma."[6]

When the family returned to Atlanta, Coretta opened a package of SCLC mail that included tapes and a threatening letter that encouraged

Martin to commit suicide. The package had been intended for delivery prior to the Nobel Prize trip, but in the volume of materials arriving at the SCLC, it had not been delivered. The tapes included edited pieces from wiretaps supposedly from Martin's hotel rooms and included evidence of acts of infidelity that could cause public humiliation if they were released. Coretta listened to the tapes, along with Martin, Ralph Abernathy, Andrew Young, Joseph Lowery, and Bernard Lee. The group assumed that the tape had been prepared by the FBI and sent on the instructions of J. Edgar Hoover. Coretta did not question Martin about the authenticity of the tapes. In an interview after Martin's death, she stated, "I just wouldn't have burdened him with anything so trivial . . . all that other business just didn't have a place in a very high-level relationship that we enjoyed."[7] Throughout the remainder of her life, Coretta continued to reject evidence that Martin had been unfaithful to her.

The business and community leaders of Atlanta had been debating about whether to recognize Martin for his accomplishments. Though interracial social or community gatherings were not common, former Mayor William Hartsfield suggested that it would be an embarrassment for the city not to do so. Coca-Cola CEO Robert Woodruff also strongly encouraged his business colleagues to buy tickets for the event, which was held at the Dinkler Hotel in January 1965. Coretta and Martin brought their children to this banquet because they had not been able to travel to Norway.

SELMA AND THE MARCH TO MONTGOMERY

While Martin worked for voting rights in Selma, Coretta traveled to visit him several times. Selma was in Dallas County, the next county over from her home of Perry County. Some activities of the Selma campaign actually occurred in Perry County, such as the murder of Jimmy Lee Jackson, who was shot after attempting to register to vote. This killing inspired SCLC worker James Bevel to call for a March to Montgomery. "We must go to Montgomery and see the king! Be prepared to sleep on the highway," he preached.[8]

Martin was arrested in Selma because of his efforts to assist African Americans in registering to vote. Coretta spoke at a mass meeting in February 1965 while Martin was in jail. She also met Malcolm X, the leader of the Nation of Islam, who had come to lend his voice to the effort.

During the Selma to Montgomery March, Coretta participated in several legs of the journey. Both she and Martin also shuttled in and out of

Alabama, as they kept speaking engagements in other states during the march.

Coretta spent the last night of the march with the group on the grounds of St. Jude's Hospital, just outside Montgomery. Harry Belafonte organized a midnight concert, and Coretta sang and recited Langston Hughes' poem "Mother to Son." The next day, the march continued into downtown Montgomery where Martin gave a speech at the state capitol.

Coretta's parents joined her on stage during Martin's speech. Her father commented, "This is the greatest day for Negroes in the history of America."[9] Coretta was also pleased, looking at the large crowd, which included both white people and African Americans. She reflected on how much had been accomplished through Martin's work and the movement. Yet, just the next day, she learned of the murder of Viola Liuzzo, a white woman from Detroit who had come to Selma and volunteered to assist the movement, reminding everyone connected with it of the distance they still had to travel.

THE BEST OF TIMES, THE WORST OF TIMES

In August 1964, the U.S. government indicated that several naval vessels had been attacked as they were conducting surveillance in the Gulf of Tonkin along the North Vietnamese coast. Word of these attacks caused Congress to pass a resolution authorizing the President to employ military force in Southeast Asia without any declaration of war. The following January President Johnson ordered the deployment of American combat troops to the region, the first time in which they had held a role other than military advisors. In March 1965, about the same time as the Selma to Montgomery March, President Johnson launched bombing campaigns against North Vietnam in an attempt to prevent the flow of men and materiel from the north to the south.

The escalation of the Vietnam War sparked the rise of the antiwar movement in the United States. More than 30 groups formed during 1965 to advocate against the war. Some of the groups involved activists who had been involved in the civil rights movement. In addition, some of the groups adapted their antiwar tactics from civil rights models, such as "teach-ins" emerging out of the "sit-in" model.

Coretta spoke out against the Vietnam War at the Emergency Peace Rally held at Madison Square Garden in New York City in June 1965. This dated her involvement in the antiwar movement almost two years prior to Martin's. Martin was reluctant to speak out initially because he saw President Johnson as an important ally for civil rights, and he did not want to endanger that relationship unnecessarily.

In fall 1965, Coretta enrolled Yolanda and Martin III in Spring Street Elementary School, an integrated school. Martin was in agreement with Coretta's actions, but he was not available at the time to handle the paperwork related to their enrollment. Juanita Abernathy also enrolled three of her children. Coretta and Martin had previously submitted applications for Yolanda and Martin III to start first grade at private schools. In both cases, they had been rejected. The Lovett School, which rejected Martin III, was affiliated with the Atlanta Diocese of the Episcopal Church, and they set a policy that they would accept no applications from African Americans, which caused a negative reaction from the national Episcopal Church.

In the summer of 1965, a riot broke out in Watts, a section of Los Angeles. Residents looted and erupted to show discontent with police brutality. Journalists and other observers noted that this social unrest was the result of frustration with the slow speed in which economic and social change was coming to their neighborhood. Though civil rights bills had been passed, schools remained crowded and inferior, citizens were unemployed, and economic opportunities were few and far between.

In 1966, in response to this outbreak of urban unrest, Martin took the SCLC into a new territory—the North. They began an antipoverty and antislums movement in Chicago. To show solidarity with the residents of Chicago, Martin moved Coretta and their children into an apartment in a dilapidated building in a poor neighborhood. During this period, Martin went to a meeting at the Nation of Islam Temple served by Elijah Muhammad. Coretta accompanied him, although she was asked to sit in the area separated for Muslim women.[10] This experience and some of the encounters that Coretta had with male civil rights leaders made her recognize the need for women's equality as well as racial equality.

In early June 1966, Coretta served as a delegate to the White House Conference "To Fulfill These Rights" organized by President Johnson. Martin also attended, although he was shuttling back and forth between Chicago and Washington. Thurgood Marshall was the keynote speaker, and he emphasized the need for adherence to the law, even in the efforts to bring about new laws. Martin felt slighted, as much of his work had of course involved nonviolent resistance to unjust laws.

That same summer, the King family returned South to participate in the "March Against Fear" in Mississippi, called by James Meredith, who had been the first African American to integrate the University of Mississippi. Meredith began this march alone on June 5, 1966, with the intention of showing that African Americans could march without protection from the U.S. government. The next day, a gunman shot Meredith soon after he crossed the Tennessee line into his home state. Civil rights groups, including CORE and SCLC, agreed to continue the march in Meredith's name, while he recovered from his wounds. Coretta, Yolanda, and Martin III participated in several legs of this march, which was met by both white resistance and calls for black power as it moved through communities such as Grenada and Philadelphia. It culminated with a rally at the state capitol in Jackson, at which James Meredith spoke.

Back in Chicago, Martin continued mobilizing for justice in housing laws. Coretta and all of the children attended a rally at Soldier Field in July 1966, and Coretta also spoke later that summer at the North Chicago YWCA. Out of this meeting an organization was formed: Women Mobilized for Change.

The Chicago movement ended after riots broke out in several neighborhoods on July 13. One cause of the riots was the oppressive heat. City officials locked fire hydrants to prevent residents from opening them and creating water attractions to cool down. Martin was away from home at the time, en route to a mass meeting. Coretta was at home with the children, and when they ran to a window to investigate a noise that they heard from the street below, she screamed at them to get away from it. This outburst led a reporter to publish the tabloid-style headline "Mrs. King Fears for her Children's Lives."[11]

Coretta was disappointed in the reporter's choice of words, but soon after the riot subsided, she returned to Atlanta with the children. Martin continued to commute to Chicago until August, when a conference, hosted by Martin and Mayor Daley, reached an agreement to provide for open access to housing in the city.

The Reverend Jesse Jackson, who had become a staffer for the SCLC during the Selma campaign, returned to Chicago(where he was in school at Chicago Theological Seminary) to initiate Operation Breadbasket in fall 1966. Operation Breadbasket allowed the SCLC to keep working against poverty in Chicago even after Martin had returned to Atlanta. After attending a program there in October 1967, Coretta suggested to Martin that they should create similar efforts in other communities.[12]

The other effort that Coretta and Martin increased in 1967 was the antiwar effort. In January 1967, Martin questioned the excess of military spending on the war in the face of poverty and inequality at home in the United States. President Johnson's escalation of the number of troops in Vietnam (which grew to 535,000 in 1967) made it difficult for the government to fund Great Society programs at home. Martin preached his first sermon devoted entirely to the Vietnam War on April 4 at the Riverside Church in New York. On April 15, Coretta spoke at a rally against the war in San Francisco, while Martin spoke at a similar rally in New York City.

In January 1968, Coretta took part in the Women's Peace Brigade march to Washington, D.C. This march was named in honor of Jeannette Rankin, the first woman to serve in the U.S. House of Representatives and the only person to vote against the U.S. entry into both World War I and World War II.[13] The Kings' increasing public visibility as antiwar caused some negative reactions because some felt that it was wrong for the movement to turn against President Johnson, who had been the person to pass civil rights legislation. Martin and Coretta's public antiwar stances also caused the FBI to increase their surveillance and to institute counter-intelligence programs (COINTELPRO) against the movement.

Later in January 1968, Coretta had to have surgery for a tumor in her abdomen. Martin stayed at home for a few days while she recovered, but he soon had to resume his travels. During this period, Coretta periodically complained to the SCLC staffers about his prolonged absences. She also worried about the lack of a trust fund for her children in the face of increased death threats against her husband. Some staff members, who sought to juggle all of the competing demands on Martin's time, nicknamed her "Queen."[14]

Martin and Coretta's last vacation together had been in 1965. In March 1968, he sent her an arrangement of artificial flowers. When asked why they were artificial, as he had traditionally sent fresh flowers, he told her that he wanted her to have a more permanent memento of his love.

In the face of conflicting demands on his time and of challenges to his leadership and philosophy, Martin re-emphasized the need for self-sacrifice and commitment to nonviolence. He and the SCLC announced plans for the Poor People's Campaign in March 1968. It would involve the creation of a tent city in Washington, D.C. that would bring together examples of poverty from Appalachia to the inner city, from the rural South to Native American reservations. This campaign would begin to address issues of economic inequity, and it would move Martin's leadership beyond the realm of seeking racial justice. To an interviewer, Martin noted, "The Black revolution is much more than a struggle for the rights of Negroes. It is forcing America to face all its interrelated flaws—racism, poverty, militarism, and materialism. It is exposing evils that are rooted deeply in the whole structure of our society. It reveals systemic rather than superficial flaws and suggests that radical reconstruction of society is the real issue to be faced."[15] His connection of racism, poverty, and militarism foreshadowed what Coretta would later call the "triple evils."

During those difficult days, Martin went to Memphis to assist in rallying support for striking sanitation workers. The vast majority of these workers were African American, so the strike had a racial significance. However, it also had an economic thrust, as the workers sought to obtain a living wage and benefits for their families, considering the dangerous nature of their tasks.

On March 23, 1968, Martin made a flight to several cities in South Georgia. He took Martin III and Dexter with him. On Friday, March 28, Coretta went to Washington to participate in a press conference with the Women's International League for Peace and Freedom. Martin came home from Memphis, depressed about how things were going there. Still, he enjoyed a fish dinner with Coretta and the Abernathys. They reflected on happier times, dating back to Montgomery, when their work together had begun. Both Martin and Coretta were very busy people by this point, though they sought to make times for the people and activities that were important to them.

NOTES

1. "King Room Exhibit," Freedom Hall, Martin Luther King, Jr. Center for Nonviolent Social Change, Atlanta, Georgia.

2. Coretta Scott King, My Life With Martin Luther King, Jr. (New York: Holt, Rinehart, Winston, 1969), 248–249.

3. "King Room," Freedom Hall.

4. King, My Life, 3–4.

5. David Garrow, Bearing the Cross: Martin Luther King, Jr. and the Southern Christian Leadership Conference (New York: Harper Collins, 1986), 355.

6. Ibid., 365.

7. Ibid., 374.

8. Taylor Branch, At Canaan's Edge: America in the King Years, 1965–1968 (New York: Simon and Schuster, 2006), 9.

9. King, My Life, 268.

10. Branch, At Canaan's Edge, 441.

11. King, My Life, 287.

12. Ibid., 290.

13. Branch, At Canaan's Edge, 673.

14. Ibid., 677–679.

15. David J. Garrow, The FBI and Martin Luther King, Jr.: From Solo to Memphis (New York: W.W. Norton & Company, 1981), 214.

Chapter 6

BECOMING A WIDOW

About 7:00 p.m. on April 4, 1968, a shot from a rifle killed Martin Luther King, Jr., in Memphis, Tennessee.

GETTING THE NEWS

Back in Atlanta, Coretta received a phone call from SCLC staffer Jesse Jackson, who informed her about the shooting and advised her to get on a plane to Memphis as soon as possible. Coretta called for Dora McDonald, Martin's secretary at the SCLC, to come and go to Memphis with her. She also broke the news of the shooting to her children. Subsequent phone calls came from Andrew Young, who advised her that Martin's situation was serious, and Mayor Ivan Allen of Atlanta, who offered his assistance.

At the Atlanta airport, a delegation of friends and family gathered. Coretta heard a page for her, and she sent Mayor Allen to respond. Dora McDonald joined her and suggested they go into the ladies lounge to sit down. Coretta later recalled that when she saw Dora's face, she knew what the news would be. Mayor Allen joined them in the lounge and broke the difficult news that Martin had died.

Coretta returned home to talk to her children. Juanita Abernathy, the Allens, and Christine and Isaac Farris were with her. The telephone began to ring incessantly. President Johnson called. Senator Robert Kennedy called to offer his assistance. He also sent the telephone company to install additional phone lines, and he arranged for a private plane for Coretta's use.

Harry Belafonte called and indicated that he was en route to Atlanta. Later, he paid for Martin's funeral. Daddy King and Mrs. King arrived, and the next day Coretta's mother and brother came from Marion, and her sister came from her home.

Making Plans and Speaking Out

The next four days were a whirlwind of activity. On April 5, Coretta, accompanied by a small group of friends and family, traveled to Memphis to claim Martin's body. They met with Ralph Abernathy, who had been with Martin in Memphis and remained there after the assassination. When they arrived back in Atlanta, approximately 300 people were on hand to pay their respects. They took Martin's body to the Hanley Funeral Home, an African American–owned firm. Coretta planned the funeral activities, with the assistance of the SCLC staff. She asked the Reverend Wyatt Tee Walker, a former SCLC director, to step in and assist, as she feared that Ralph Abernathy was at the point of exhaustion.

The SCLC staff also assisted Coretta in organizing a meeting with the press, and she made her first public comment the evening of April 6. Bernard Lee, who had been Martin's special assistant, introduced Ralph Abernathy, who introduced Coretta. Coretta spoke briefly and did not take any questions from the reporters who were in attendance.

Coretta's first words were to thank Ralph Abernathy, whom she deemed "my husband's closest friend and associate." She then indicated that it had always been Martin's belief that if anything happened to him, he would want Ralph to assume leadership of the SCLC, for "Dr. Abernathy could express and interpret his views on nonviolence better than anyone else and would know how he wanted things to carry on."[1]

Coretta wore a simple black dress and no hat or veil. Her voice remained subdued throughout the statement, and she spoke in an Alabama drawl. She was obviously upset and tired, but her face was stoic. She began her prepared statement with the words, "I would have preferred to be at home at this time with my children." She came forward to speak publicly "because thousands of people have asked how they can best carry on his work. So once again I have put aside traditional family considerations because my husband's wish for his people, for all poor people, transcends my wish for privacy."[2]

She only referred to Martin once by name, "We were always willing to share Martin Luther King with the world because he was a symbol of the finest man is capable of being." The rest of the time, she called him "my husband" or referred to him in the third person. The most unusual, detached sentence of the press conference was, "And so he's gone, but we have Ralph Abernathy, Andrew Young, Bernard Lee, and so many others to carry on his work."

Coretta began what would be a common theme for her: Martin's work must go on. "Our concern is that his work does not die. He gave his life for the poor of the world, the garbage workers of Memphis and the peasants of Vietnam. Nothing hurt more than the thought that man could attempt no way to solve problems except by violence." She also asserted that "we intend to go on . . . and I hope that you who loved and admired him will join us in fulfilling his dream."[3] It was a call to commemoration, a call to nonviolence, and a call to action toward the establishment of a more just world.

Martin's body was also moved to Sisters Chapel on the Spelman College campus on April 6 for a period of viewing by the public. The family and friends went in first. Xernona Clayton, an SCLC staffer, was shocked at the appearance of his jaw, which had been damaged by the gun shot. She borrowed powder from Mrs. King and Julie Belafonte (Harry's wife) and mixed up a paste, in an attempt to cover the wound. She recalled that "Coretta smiled" when she saw this improvement.[4] Over the next two days, an estimated 60,000 people joined the family in paying final respects.

While the public viewing was underway, the King household remained a flurry of activity. Xernona Clayton obtained dresses and veils for Coretta and the other women to wear to the funeral. Hosea Williams and other SCLC staff members found the mule drawn wagon that would carry Martin's body between Ebenezer (where the private, religious service would be held) and Morehouse (where the open air service for the public would be held).

RETURN TO MEMPHIS

On April 8, Coretta, Harry Belafonte, Yolanda, Martin III, and Dexter flew to Memphis to participate in a nonviolent march with the striking sanitation workers that Martin had been prepared to lead prior to his death. The family held hands and led the integrated march that included SCLC staffers and union officials. It was drizzling rain, and it took approximately two hours for the crowd (which estimates numbered at between 6,000 and 12,500) to march to City Hall, where a rally occurred.

The *Atlanta Constitution* noted that Coretta appeared fatigued and was "fighting a head cold." They also noted that she marched with half-closed eyes and lips that appeared fixed in a slightly nervous half-smile.[5]

In spite of her pain, Coretta gave a speech that moved the crowd. She reminded them of Martin's sacrifice, as well as of the sacrifice that she and her children had shared. She also noted that she had always been his partner in the movement, who stood in for him when he asked. Even in the midst of this difficult circumstance, she would continue to work toward the fulfillment of Martin's efforts for justice and equality.

Then she used an analogy reminiscent of a minister's sermon:

> And those of you who believe in what Martin Luther King, Jr. stood for, I would challenge you today to see that his spirit never dies and that we will go forward from this experience, which to me represents the crucifixion, on towards the resurrection and the redemption of the spirit.
>
> How many times have I heard him say, that with every Good Friday there comes Easter? When Good Friday comes there are the moments in life when we feel that all is lost, and there is no hope. But then Easter comes as a time of resurrection, of rebirth, or hope, and fulfillment.[6]

She recounted the work of the civil rights movement that her husband had been involved in, from the Montgomery Bus Boycott, to the Selma Campaign for Voting Rights, to the concerns for economic justice, which had brought him to Memphis. She affirmed that the planned Poor People's Campaign would become a reality, and then she added that the concerns about economics were not only restricted to African Americans in the United States. "We are concerned about not only the Negro poor, but the poor all over America and all over the world."[7]

She closed with a note of concern about the violence in society, manifested by both the domestic unrest that was starting across the country in the aftermath of Dr. King's assassination and perhaps in the war in Vietnam. "But then I ask the question: How many men must die before we can really have a free and true and peaceful society? How long will it take?"[8]

The speech focused on resistance to racism, calls for economic justices, and opposition to war and violence. These three themes continued as primary focuses for Coretta throughout the remainder of her life, and she often referred to them as the "triple evils of racism, poverty, and violence."

ATLANTA AND OTHER CITIES RESPOND

Back in Atlanta, political dignitaries poured in from across the United States and around the world for the funeral. Celebrities also descended on Atlanta. Coretta recalled that one visit that meant a lot to her was by Bill Cosby and Robert Culp of the television show "I Spy," who played with her children.

In the aftermath of the assassination, riots broke out in 130 cities across the United States. Washington, D.C. was one of the hardest hit, with nine people being killed. Despite their anger and sadness at the situation, Atlantans maintained order during the period. Churches with white membership, such as Central Presbyterian, opened their doors to feed and house out-of-town mourners. The Atlanta Transit Authority also operated for free during the period.

THE FUNERAL

Mayor Ivan Allen declared April 9 to be a day of mourning in Atlanta. On the other hand, Governor Lester Maddox refused to close the State Capitol and installed state troopers around the perimeter of it.

At the King home, Kathryn Johnson, a white AP reporter, cooked breakfast for the children and other visitors. Jacqueline Kennedy came by the house to pay her respects. Kathryn Johnson recalled that she "made a beeline for me and shook my hands: I know she thought I was the Kings' white maid."[9]

June Dobbs Butts, sister of Maynard Jackson, who would later be the first African American mayor of Atlanta, recalled a scene of Jacqueline Kennedy, Betty Shabazz, and Coretta standing together at the services, three widows.[10] Over the rest of her life, Coretta was associated among this group of widows from the 1960s, along with Myrlie Evers-Williams.

At Ebenezer church there was an overflowing crowd, even though this was supposed to be a private service. Stokely Carmichael, who had been an early leader of SNCC, protested that he was not being allowed in, while white dignitaries were. When he was allowed into the church, he came to the front and kneeled beside Coretta to talk to her. Coretta told him, "Martin wouldn't want you to do that," in an attempt to prevent any further provocations or appeals to Carmichael's philosophy of black power.[11]

Ralph Abernathy presided over the service at Ebenezer. It included prayers, scripture, and favorite hymns. Martin's major professor from Boston University, Dr. Harold DeWolf, offered a tribute. Coretta held five-year-old Bernice on her lap during the service. Monetta Sleet, an African American journalist, captured this scene in a photograph that later won the Pulitzer Prize. Prior to the service, Coretta had intervened to gain him access to the church.

The service closed with a tape being played of one of Martin's sermons, "The Drum Major Instinct." While Coretta had attempted to explain to her children that they would hear his voice but would not be able to talk to him any more, it was a difficult moment for the children. In conjunction with the fortieth anniversary of the assassination, Bernice King recalled, "I was looking around—where is he? Of course, he was dead. I remember that specifically. It was traumatic."[12]

After the first service, the processional marched 30 blocks across town to the Morehouse campus. Martin's casket was carried in a rough wooden cart drawn by two mules. Coretta and the children began the walk with the group but later rode the rest of the way in a car. It was a sunny day, approximately 80 degrees.

Because of concerns about the heat and the length of the services, the family asked that the political dignitaries not give verbal tributes during the section at Morehouse. This caused some upset when dignitaries did not get to offer their planned remarks. However, the service still included prayer, hymns, and scripture, as well as multiple other speakers. Benjamin Mays, who had been president of Morehouse when Martin was a student, gave the eulogy. Mahalia Jackson sang Thomas Dorsey's classic "Precious Lord, Take My Hand." The service ran over-time, and there was concern that it would soon rain, which would be disastrous for the outdoor gathering.

Following the Morehouse service, there was a private burial at South-view cemetery. By this point, the events had lasted seven hours. Rain and thunderstorms began shortly after the burial.

NOTES

1. "WSB-TV news film clip of Coretta Scott King following the assassination of her husband, Dr. Martin Luther King, Jr., speaking at a press conference held at Ebenezer Baptist Church, Atlanta, Georgia, 1968 April 6," WSB-TV news film collection, reel 1455, 21:14/34:39, Walter J. Brown Media Archives and Peabody Award Collection, The University of Georgia Libraries, Athens, GA, http://www.crdl.usg.edu.

2. Ibid.

3. Ibid.

4. Rebecca Burns, "King: an Oral History," *Atlanta Magazine*, April 2008, 134.

5. Austin Scott, "Widow of King Leads March in Quiet Memphis," *Atlanta Constitution*, April 9, 1968, A-14.

6. Coretta Scott King, *My Life With Martin Luther King, Jr.* (New York: Holt, Rinehart, Winston, 1969), 345.

7. Ibid., 346.

8. Ibid., 347.

9. Burns, 138.

10. Ibid.

11. Jim Auchumutey, "We Lost a Hero But Kept the Peace," *Atlanta Journal-Constitution*, March 30, 2008, A-10.

12. Burns, 141.

Chapter 7

ESTABLISHING HIS AND HER LEGACY: THE KING CENTER

On April 11, 1968, Coretta met with Mayor Ivan Allen to discuss plans for a memorial to Martin in Atlanta. She also set up an office at her home. The care of her children remained her primary concern, although she also had a strong desire to continue to work for social and economic justice, as well as to preserve the memory of Martin. Martin's life had been full with a variety of home and work duties, and Coretta intended to follow in his footsteps.

Coretta's vision of how to memorialize Martin included several components. She felt strongly that the neighborhood in which he grew up and worked should be preserved and enhanced as tourist attractions. She also intended to collect and use his writings and those of other civil rights groups to preserve the stories of the movement. In addition, she wanted to promote Martin's philosophy of nonviolence and to suggest how his tactics could apply to contemporary issues. Over the next 15 years, Coretta was the driving force behind bringing each of these memorials into existence.

CORETTA AND THE SCLC

In the aftermath of the funeral, letters and sympathy cards poured into the SCLC office for Coretta and the rest of the family. Many of them included checks, and some of the checks were made out to Coretta. Nonetheless, following the practice that Martin had begun during his life, SCLC maintained these funds for the organization rather than passing them directly to Coretta. This decision increased the tensions between Coretta and some of Martin's SCLC colleagues. On the other hand, deputies such as Andrew Young began to act as surrogate fathers to the King children.

On April 13, 1968, Coretta was elected to the SCLC Board. She also agreed to participate in the upcoming Poor People's Campaign. The *Atlanta Constitution* noted that "her election to the board apparently reflects the SCLC aim to use her as a rallying point following the slaying of her husband."[1] Andrew Young's memoir *An Easy Burden* echoed those sentiments, noting that SCLC sought to use her to raise funds for the SCLC, but they did not want her to play any policy role in the organization.[2] On the other hand, Ralph Abernathy's memoir *And the Walls Came Tumbling Down* presented a different story:

> After the funeral and readjustment to life without him, Coretta decided to build a center in memory of Martin, an institution to carry on his work. I had encouraged her to become active in the SCLC and had even prepared an office for her in our headquarters. But she wanted to pursue the future independently, and certainly there were many donors who were eager to contribute to a fitting memorial for Martin. So with seventy-five thousand dollars from the Ebenezer Baptist Church and *seventy-five thousand dollars that the SCLC contributed* [emphasis added], she bought a piece of property next door to the Ebenezer Church, and went forward with plans to build the Martin Luther King, Jr. Center for Nonviolent Social Change.[3]

Andrew Young elaborated on Coretta's motivations:

> While Martin had often talked about his death, he made no provisions for Coretta and the children. Now, money was coming in as a result of Martin's death and Coretta needed it for the family. But there was no sensitivity to that among Ralph [Abernathy] and many SCLC Board members . . . There were a lot of contestants for Martin's legacy, and Coretta wanted to take up the mantle, too. She had always seen herself as a civil rights leader, not just as a wife in the background . . . But Coretta had come into her own when she began representing Martin at rallies and demonstrations against the war in Vietnam. Martin could keep her 'in her place' so to speak, but there was no way Ralph, Joe Lowery, Hosea Williams, or any of us were going to tell Coretta what to do. She was determined to do more than raise children. She was committed to seeing that her husband's work was carried on.[4]

Coretta did not speak out publicly at the time as to her reasons for developing the King Center as an independent organization. She also remained close to and continued to work with both Ralph Abernathy and Andrew Young over the years, despite any differences of opinion about Martin's legacy. In addition, the Abernathys were involved in events at the King Center, and Coretta and her children were involved with activities with the SCLC. There were also occasional public disagreements, especially around the time that Ralph published his memoir in 1989, but due to the loyalty that grew out of the relationship between Martin and Ralph, the families never broke completely.

In 1993, in an interview with the *Atlanta Constitution*, Coretta admitted her claims to leadership. "There are a lot of people who would love to relegate me to a symbolic figure and that's it. I have never been just a symbol of anything. I am a thinker. I have strong beliefs and I try to be an example of what I believe in."[5] Her efforts in building the King Center demonstrated her commitment to leadership and to service in the causes about which she was committed.

CORETTA TAKES STANDS

Coretta's earliest public appearances following the funeral were part peace and antipoverty rallies. On April 27, 1968, Coretta fulfilled a commitment for Martin and spoke at a peace rally in New York's Central Park. Coretta began, "I come to New York today with a strong feeling that my dearly beloved husband, who was snatched suddenly from our midst slightly more than three weeks ago now, would have wanted me to be present today. Though my heart is heavy with grief from having suffered an irreparable loss, my faith in the redemptive will of God is stronger today than ever before."[6] The speech also included "Ten Commandments on Vietnam," which were points that she found among Martin's papers. On Mother's Day, she participated in a March for Welfare Rights and gave the keynote address.

The SCLC implemented the Poor People's March on Washington in June, but the Poor People's Campaign was not an overwhelming success. The SCLC built a shantytown, called Resurrection City, on the National Mall. The community lacked adequate electricity, water, or sanitation, and after it rained, the area became a sea of mud. Approximately 2,500 people stayed in the area during the Campaign, with on average about 500 living there at a single time. Some Mexican American and Native American leaders clashed with the SCLC organizers, accusing them of dominating the effort, which was supposed to be multiethnic.

Coretta spoke during a rally on June 19 and called for women to mobilize a campaign of conscience against the "triple evils" of poverty, racism, and war. The phrase "triple evils" was a common theme in Coretta's speeches for the rest of her life. Coretta also shared a telegram from Ethel Kennedy, the widow of Robert Kennedy, who had been assassinated on June 5, 1968. She noted, "We have come to realize the broad dimensions of violence in our society by the tragic loss of two men."[7] Soon after this rally, Capitol police insisted that the shantytown residents leave the area.

On June 26, 1968, Coretta announced the incorporation of the entity that would become the Martin Luther King, Jr. Center for Nonviolent Social Change. She began fundraising and obtained a first grant from the Rockefeller Foundation. Over the years, Coretta's fundraising efforts tapped into individual, corporate, and foundation sources, as well as city, state, and federal government grants for programs and infrastructure. Coretta's vision and ideas remained central to the planning and direction of the King Center and its activities, and her personal involvement was a key to the fundraising successes that it had.

MAKING A LIVING AND
RAISING FUNDS FOR THE CENTER

Also in July 1968, Coretta went into seclusion in New Hampshire to write her memoir *My Life with Martin Luther King, Jr.* This book was published in 1969 and became a best seller, and royalties provided income for the family. Coretta also began to travel for speaking engagements and fundraising. Her sister, Edythe, moved to Atlanta and provided assistance with the children.

After a turbulent political season caused by public outcry against the Vietnam War and distress about the assassinations of Martin and Robert Kennedy, Richard Nixon was elected president in November 1968. He received only 500,000 votes more than Democrat Hubert Humphrey, but he won the electoral college by a margin of 301 to 191. Independent candidate George Wallace was also a factor, gaining almost 10,000,000 popular votes and 46 electoral votes. While the Republicans had taken the White House, the Democrats remained in control of both houses of Congress. This set the stage for a battle over the continuation of the Great Society social welfare programs that President Johnson had established. In addition, there were an increasing number of groups seeking to have their rights established and recognized, and this gave Coretta and the King Center more areas on which to work.

In fall 1968, Coretta announced that the initial efforts of the Center would focus on collecting the papers of Martin, the SCLC, and other major civil rights organizations. At the first commemorative service, in January 1969, she announced plans to move Martin's body to a memorial on Auburn Avenue and to build a complex for the King Center there. Her plans for the King Center included the development of a research and educational unit, the Institute for African American Studies, as well as the Institute for Nonviolent Social Change.

During 1969, Coretta traveled a great deal. She visited Italy, and their government presented her an award. She also visited India again and accepted the posthumous presentation of the Nehru Award to Martin. On March 17, she preached at St. Paul's Cathedral in London, possibly the first time a woman had been allowed to do such. She also received honorary degrees from Boston University, Brandeis University, and Marymount College and held a fellowship at Yale University. The International Overseas Foundation presented her the "Pacem in Terra" Award, and SANE (an anti–nuclear weapons group) presented her the Eleanor Roosevelt Award. She became a recognized personality and spokesperson across the United States and the world, and these opportunities enabled her to raise more funds for the King Center.

In 1970, the board of the King Center held its first meeting and announced the establishment of the Institute for the Black World. It was located on the campus of the Atlanta University Center, and the director was Dr. Vincent Harding. This focus on African American Studies within a national and international context connected to trends in academic research and scholarship of the era. Emerging partially from the civil rights movement, there was increased focus on acknowledging the contributions of African Americans and also on identifying elements of African American culture that reflected African roots.

Also in January 1970, Martin's body was moved and reburied in a crypt adjacent to Ebenezer. People and tourists began to visit the gravesite, and Coretta recognized its potential as the center of a shrine.

Coretta continued to travel, this time to promote her book. Everywhere she went, people lined up to catch a glimpse of her. During a European tour, she did a Freedom Concert in Amsterdam.

During this period, she also authorized filmmaker Eli Landau to develop a documentary, *King: A Filmed Record from Montgomery to Memphis*, which was another fundraiser for the King Center. Like her involvement in preserving Martin's papers, the development of this film inserted her views and control into the presentation of Martin's life and work for history.

THE KING CENTER AND NEIGHBORHOOD DEVELOPMENT

Coretta remained an ally to mayors of Atlanta. Sam Massell, the first Jewish person to serve as mayor, was elected in 1969. Via a federal–city funding relationship, Atlanta built a public housing project called the Martin Luther King, Jr. Village in Southeast Atlanta. Coretta and her children participated in the groundbreaking on King Day 1969 and the dedication on King Day 1971.

In the late 1960s and early 1970s, Americans perceived that there was an increase in crime, due to social unrest and also the continuing war in Vietnam. Due to her commitment to spreading Martin's view on nonviolence, Coretta determined that there was a role for the King Center in responding to these concerns. The 1970s also saw a proliferation of research institutes and think tanks at universities and other nonprofit organizations. Coretta developed plans for the Institute for Nonviolence at the King Center during 1970–71. With the research center came opportunities to apply for grants and seek foundation funding. The first conference on nonviolence was in 1971, and it produced a report. The King Center also developed a project to counter violence in the schools, and in 1972 they received a grant from the National Institutes of Health to focus on violence in factories.

Other opportunities for fundraising were connected to the commemoration of Martin's birthday, which the King Center organized. In 1973, the King Center presented the first Martin Luther King Jr. Peace Prize to Andrew Young, who was then serving as a Congressman.

In 1972, Coretta began serving on the planning commission for presidential elections, a joint effort between the Democratic and Republican parties that scheduled dates for primaries and conventions, as well as organized debates. The need for this commission grew out of the fact that the branches of government were divided in party loyalty. In addition, the 1970s saw an increase in television coverage of campaigns and elected officials, so there was a need to control how the media would interact with candidates. Coretta continued to serve on these commissions until 1984.

In 1973, Atlanta elected its first African American mayor, Maynard Jackson. Under his administration, city support for the development of the King site increased. Additional public support came through Fulton County. Also in 1973, the U.S. Department of Housing and Urban Development awarded a grant for a park and community center to be across the street from the King crypt. Atlanta's Robert Woodruff Foundation made an anonymous $1 million gift toward the effort. Alpha Kappa Alpha Sorority raised funds to purchase the King birth home from Martin's mother so that it could become a museum. Lobbying began to have the stretch of Auburn Avenue between Ebenezer and the birth home declared a national historic district.

Also in 1973, the King Center sponsored its first oral history conference, which allowed scholars to begin to capture the stories of civil rights movement veterans. Some movement veterans, such as Hosea Williams, began to question Coretta's plans and extensive fundraising, again noting Martin's example of giving to the SCLC. However, the King Center efforts went forward. On King Day in 1974, a $10 million capital campaign kicked off to construct a complex of buildings designed by architectural firm Bond, Ryder, James, a firm with African American principals. Georgia Governor Jimmy Carter mounted a portrait of Martin in the capitol building on February 17, 1974, and Coretta and a large audience of politicians and civil rights activists presided over the ceremony, which ended with the group singing "We Shall Overcome." That same year, Governor Carter had noted, "Georgia is a better state and the South is a greater nation for what he [Martin] did."[8]

Ground was broken for an interfaith chapel and permanent entombment around the crypt in 1975. Atlanta Gas Light Company installed an "eternal flame," similar to the one that burns at John F. Kennedy's grave in Arlington Cemetery. Also in 1975, the restored birth home opened as a museum.

Throughout the fundraising campaigns for the King Center, Coretta focused on continuing awareness of Martin's work and philosophy and its implications for the future. She also maintained relationships with movement allies, such as labor unions, who were regular donors to the King Center. In 1974, the King Center presented its nonviolent peace prize to César Chávez, leader of the United Farm Workers. Coretta made the presentation during a benefit concert for the King Center. Chávez noted that "Dr. King was really our teacher. His life and deeds and his teachings continue to grow. Among us, they are goals to strive for."[9] In 1976, the King Center inaugurated an annual "Labor-Management Social Responsibility Breakfast" as part of the birthday observances.

Another group with which Coretta collaborated in the mid-1970s was the National Education Association. In summer 1976, the King Center offered a summer institute on nonviolence to train educators and young people in Martin's philosophy and techniques.

A GEORGIAN IN THE WHITE HOUSE

In November 1976, Governor Jimmy Carter was elected President of the United States. Coretta and Daddy King both supported his candidacy during the campaign, and she also served on the committee to plan events surrounding his inauguration. Coretta recognized advantages in having a

Georgian in the White House, and she regularly contacted the administration with requests and to pass along resumes of candidates for appointments and government jobs. Along with other African American leaders, she strongly encouraged President Carter to appoint more African Americans to the federal judiciary. She also sought to identify opportunities for the King Center to apply for and receive grants and contracts.

President Carter agreed to serve as an honorary chairperson for the ecumenical services on Martin's birthday during each year of his term. While he could not actually attend the event each year, he sent official greetings for inclusion in the program, and he also often sent representatives of his office.

In March 1977, President Carter appointed Coretta to serve on the National Commission on the Observance of International Women's Year. In July 1977, President Carter presented the Presidential Medal of Freedom posthumously to Martin, and Coretta accepted on his behalf. The other recipient on this evening was Dr. Jonas Salk. It was a small ceremony, attended by the recipients and their family members, as well as about 25 members of Congress.

In September 1977, President Carter appointed Coretta to serve as one of the public delegates to the United Nations. At the time, Andrew Young served as the Ambassador to the United Nations, the first African American to hold this post. He resigned from the post in 1979, after a controversial meeting with representatives of the Palestinian Liberation Organization. President Carter appointed Donald McHenry to succeed him. However, he also received several letters from members of the public who suggested that Coretta would be an appropriate choice.

In 1978, the National Endowment for the Humanities awarded a grant to the King Center for the processing and preservation of papers of Martin and the SCLC. Funds underwrote an archival consultant to begin organizing the materials for publication.

In October 1978, President and Mrs. Carter hosted a reception for Friends of the King Center at the White House. It was in conjunction with a capital campaign. Coretta sang, performing part of the material she had developed for the Freedom Concerts. Approximately 100 business, religious, and governmental leaders attended.

The second capital campaign, which had been inaugurated in 1977 by industrialist Henry Ford II, sought to raise funds to build Freedom Hall, which would contain an auditorium, gift shop, and classrooms, on the corner of Auburn Avenue and Boulevard. The Ford Motor Company pledged $1 million, and the United Auto Workers provided $600,000.

Ironically, while Coretta was raising funds from industries and unions, the focus of the King observances in 1977 and 1978 tied into concerns about unemployment. In the 1977 "State of the Dream" speech, Coretta noted that unemployment was the nation's foremost problem.[10] At the 1978 service, Benjamin Mays called for full employment, and Coretta said full employment would solve the "transcendent social problems" of the 1970s.[11] During this era, Coretta was also active in advocating for the passage of the Humphrey-Hawkins full employment bill. She cochaired the Full Employment Action Council with Murray Finley of the Amalgamated Clothing Workers Union, a branch of the AFL-CIO. In August 1978, they met with President Carter on behalf of the bill.

Another major concern of Coretta's during this era was the rights of women and families. She advocated passage of the Equal Rights Amendment. She also participated in the 1977 National Women's Conference, sending recommendations to Congress and the President about women's status, and President Carter appointed Coretta to be Deputy Chairman of the White House Conference on Families. In 1980, Coretta received the "Outstanding Mother Award" from the National Mother's Day Committee.

In October 1978, Coretta traveled to Montgomery to speak in conjunction with the renaming of Dexter Avenue Baptist Church as Dexter Avenue King Memorial Baptist Church. The previous year the church had celebrated its centennial of service, and it had also been designated a National Historic Landmark by the National Park Service, mainly due to its association with Martin's legacy. In her speech, Coretta noted, "My husband was able to translate God's love into action by trying to change the social order." She also called on the congregation to "live up to [Martin's] example as the church embraces his name. Do not use his name, as some have done, without regard to his philosophy."[12]

Also in 1980, Congress enacted law to establish the Martin Luther King Jr. Historic Site and preservation district, and President Carter signed the law. In 1981, the King Center moved its offices into the complex on Auburn Avenue. In October of that year, the archives opened for research. Freedom Hall was dedicated on King Day 1982. In 1984, the King Center retired $10 million in indebtedness on the complex, using donations from IBM, Coca-Cola, Disney, Southern Bell, Xerox, and the National Education Association. The U.S. government provided $4 million, and funds came from Kuwait and Saudi Arabia.[13]

THE KING HOLIDAY—INITIAL EFFORTS

On April 8, 1968, Representative John Conyers, an African American Democrat from Michigan, introduced legislation in the U.S. Congress to establish a federal holiday on January 15, Martin's birthday. Another major effort of Coretta's was advocating for the passing of this holiday, and she persevered in her efforts for the next 15 years.

U.S. Senator Edward Brooke, an African American Republican from Massachusetts, also introduced a bill in 1968 calling for the President to issue a proclamation annually that declared January 15 as "Martin Luther King, Jr. Day." Brooke suggested that the Presidential proclamations should urge citizens to remember Martin's service to the country and to mark the day with honors, ceremonies, and prayers. Under Brooke's resolution, the day would be a national day of commemoration, but not a federal holiday.

On January 15, 1969, the King Center hosted its first commemorative service, instituting a pattern similar to the one described in Brooke's resolution. Representative John Conyers participated in this service, as did Cleveland Robinson, the leader of the Distributive Workers of America, a labor union. Robinson was a friend of Coretta's. He stated, "We don't want anyone to believe we hope Congress will do this. We're just sayin', us Black people in America just ain't gonna work on that day anymore."[14]

As Robinson predicted, the support of labor unions and their members was important to increasing support for the establishment of the holiday. As early as 1969, a small group of workers at a General Motors plant in New York refused to work on King's birthday. That same fall a few thousand New York City hospital workers went on strike, and one of the concessions that ensured their return to work was the promise of a paid holiday on King's birthday. During the 1970s, additional unions, including those of public employees and teachers, negotiated to include the holiday in their labor contracts.

Another group that contributed substantially to promoting the holiday was the Congressional Black Caucus (CBC), which formed in 1971. Each Congressional session, Representative Conyers and Senator Brooke resubmitted versions of their bills. The CBC assisted them in gaining additional cosponsors and participated in other efforts to advocate for the holiday. Coretta coordinated her own lobbying efforts through the CBC.

ENLISTING ALLIES

Coretta also worked with the SCLC. In 1971, they launched a petition drive in support of the holiday. After a variety of local SCLC affiliates collected signatures, they garnered the support of 3,000,000 citizens and presented their case to Congress. Nonetheless, Congress did not vote on the bills.

While Coretta and her allies continued to work toward the establishment of a federal holiday, some state governments took local action. In

1973, Illinois enacted the first state King Holiday bill, via a bill introduced by Chicagoan Harold Washington. In 1974, Massachusetts and Connecticut legislators voted to establish the holiday in their states. In 1975, the New Jersey Supreme Court determined that its state was required to offer a paid holiday in honor of Martin, per the state government's contract with their employees.

Coretta saw hope for federal action via the candidacy and election of Georgian Jimmy Carter as President. During the campaign, he had indicated to labor leaders that he would support the legislation. Coretta continued to lobby him and to call for full employment in King Day celebrations. However, the economic difficulties of the era made him less willing and able to support expensive government programs.

In 1978, the National Council of Churches called on Congress to pass the holiday. In 1979, President Carter included advocacy for the holiday in the written text of his State of the Union, but he omitted to include a statement of support from his oral presentation presented to the joint session of Congress.

COMING CLOSER

The year 1979 also marked the 50th anniversary of Martin's birth. Coretta and the King Center decided to use this anniversary to launch a new effort to garner support for the holiday. They coordinated additional citizen advocacy, including another petition drive. In January, Coretta presented President Carter with the seventh annual King Center Nonviolent Peace Prize. That same year, President Carter called for the U.S. Post Office to issue a commemorative stamp to honor Martin on what would have been his 50th birthday.

Congressman Conyers continued to reintroduce his bill and to gain cosponsors. Finally, Congressional committees began to review the bill. Coretta testified before the Senate Judiciary Committee on February 19, and on March 27, she testified before a joint Congressional hearing. Additional hearings were held on June 21.

The bill came to the floor of the House of Representatives on November 13, via a procedure called suspension of the rules. This format limited the time for debate to 40 minutes (with 20 in favor and 20 opposed). Representative Conyers managed the debate for those in favor, and Rep. Gene Taylor, a Republican from Missouri, managed the debate for those opposed. His primary argument was that the country's economic situation would not allow the "luxury of another $212 million Federal holiday."[15] Conyers responded that the decision on the bill "will indicate the kind of moral direction of our country in the coming years. Congress will have to make the most positive statement it can that the sectional and racial chapter of America's history has been closed forever."[16]

Though the debate period was short, 18 Congressmen spoke, including 7 members of the Congressional Black Caucus. In the end, 252 members voted for the bill, and 133 were opposed, meaning that the bill failed to pass due to the lack of a two-thirds majority.

Congress passed a special rule to allow reconsideration of the bill later in the session. A representative introduced an amendment to change the holiday from January 15 to the third Monday in January. Another amendment, designed to save funds, suggested the holiday be the third Sunday in January. After both amendments passed, the managers moved that the bill be suspended. It was never brought up again during the session, and the Senate also did not bring up a resolution introduced by Senator Birch Bayh of Indiana, which the Judiciary Committee had reported to the floor. The head of the CBC, Representative Cardiss Collins, criticized President Carter for failing to round up the votes needed for the holiday to pass.

Economic concerns obviously played a role in the failure of the King Holiday to pass during President Carter's administration. Coretta remained an ally of the administration, and the president invited her to attend the signing ceremony for the Egyptian–Israeli peace pact on March 26, 1979 (the day before she testified about the King Holiday). President Carter also had a 15-minute meeting with Martin III on November 5 "to discuss his future and career." President Carter called Coretta that evening and reached her the next morning to give her an update on their conversation.[17] This was in the midst of the beginning of the Iran crisis, as the American Embassy in Tehran had been overrun on November 4. The fact that President Carter made time for this appointment and call reflected the value he placed on maintaining a good relationship with Coretta and her family.

In early 1980, singer Stevie Wonder released "Happy Birthday," a recording in honor of Martin and a fundraiser for the holiday effort. The Kings also worked for President Carter's re-election campaign during 1980. Coretta seconded his nomination at the Democratic National Convention in New York City. That visible political alignment caused some difficulties for the Holiday effort once President Reagan was elected in November 1980.

President Carter continued to receive letters from the public suggesting that he declare the King Holiday even after his defeat for re-election. To these writers, the holiday was a bit of unfinished business that needed resolution.

During the 97th Congress, House and Senate committees continued to hold hearings on the holiday, but neither of the bills came up for a vote. Coretta wrote a series of letters to mayors, governors, city council members, and other elected officials urging them to pass resolutions in support of the holiday. She built a collection of such resolutions in the archives at the King Center, and she also used the materials in lobbying Congress.

In 1982, Coretta also connected advocacy for the holiday to preparation for the 20th anniversary of the March on Washington. Stevie Wonder continued to support the effort, providing funds for a lobbying office in Washington, D.C., and Coretta and Stevie Wonder took petitions to House Speaker Tip O'Neill containing more than 6,000,000 signatures.

LAST STRUGGLES

Although there were still obstacles to overcome, 1983 was the year of success. Representative Conyers obtained a record number of 176 cosponsors for the bill. Senator Charles "Mac" Mathias, a Republican from Maryland, introduced a companion bill in the Senate.

Hearings began on the bill in the House in June, and Coretta arrived to testify once again. Representative Katie Hall, a freshman Democrat from Indiana, managed the bill, with full backing of Representative Conyers and the Congressional Black Caucus. This bill designated the holiday as the third Monday in January.

Debate began on August 2, 1983. A total of 48 representatives spoke about the bill, the largest number that had ever been involved in debate on this topic. Opponents of the bill continued to question the cost of another holiday, but leaders from both parties provided responses to counter that argument.

Republicans who provided support included Jack Kemp and Newt Gingrich. Kemp noted that it was important for Republicans to support the holiday, to manifest their continuing connection to working for freedom, as demonstrated by President Abraham Lincoln, one of their founding fathers. In addition, he noted that the bill would commemorate the civil rights movement and that this was important for America to do as another way of showing its commitment to core principles of equality and human dignity.

Representative John Conyers added, "I have never viewed it as an isolated piece of legislation to honor one man. Rather I have always viewed it as an indication of the commitment of the House and the Nation to the dream of Dr. King. When we pass this legislation, we should signal our commitment to the realization of full employment, world peace, and freedom for all."[18]

In a rare instance of taking the well to speak in relation to a bill, Speaker Tip O'Neill endorsed the legislation and closed the debate. He received a standing ovation. After that, the bill passed 338–90, well beyond the number needed to override a veto, if necessary.

The bill moved on to the Senate. Supporters made a large push for the bill in conjunction with the 20th anniversary of the March on Washington. Also, in anticipation of opposition in the Senate, Coretta, Martin III, and many other supporters held a prayer vigil outside the Capitol.

A challenge on the Senate side was the opposition of Senator Jesse Helms (R-N.C.), who mounted a filibuster against the bill. Helms disapproved of the idea of a holiday to honor Martin because he believed some of the ideas suggested by FBI surveillance reports, including that Martin associated with communists and otherwise demonstrated moral lapses during civil rights trips. Through negotiation, Republican Senate leaders convinced Helms to end his filibuster on October 5, 1983. Still, he shared with colleagues information from FBI files designed to impugn Martin's character.

When the bill came to the floor, Senator Ted Kennedy criticized Helms for engaging in such personal attacks. Senator Howard Baker (the Republican Majority Leader from Tennessee) moderated between the sides. Senator Daniel Patrick Moynihan (D-N.Y.) and Senator Bill Bradley (D-N.J.) also spoke strongly on behalf of the bill. After two days of debate, it passed, 78–22. The same day, President Reagan announced his intent to sign the bill when it reached his desk.

President Ronald Reagan signed Public Law 98-144 on November 2, 1983. Coretta was beside him on this day in the White House Rose Garden. In his remarks, President Reagan praised Martin's work in the civil rights movement. He also praised Coretta and Daddy King for their efforts in continuing Martin's work.

The first national celebration did not occur until 1986, and it was not until 1999 that the last state recognized the federal holiday. Still, the passing of this law marked a milestone in the establishment of Martin's legacy. He became the first African American in American history to have a holiday designated in his honor. As Michael Eric Dyson notes in *Why I Love Black Women*, "Without Coretta Scott King's tireless efforts, her husband's legacy might note have as quickly garnered national, indeed global acceptance."[19]

NOTES

1. Alex Coffin, "Mrs. King to Participate in Washington Protest," *Atlanta Constitution*, April 13, 1968, 1, 12.

2. Andrew Young, *An Easy Burden: The Civil Rights Movement and the Transformation of America* (New York: Harper Collins, 1996), 479.

3. Ralph David Abernathy, *And the Walls Came Tumbling Down: An Autobiography* (New York: Harper Collins, 1989), 465.

4. Young, 479.

5. Gary Pomerantz, "Interview Coretta Scott King: 'I have never been just a symbol,' " *Atlanta Constitution*, January 17, 1993, A1, A12.

6. Octavia Vivian, *Coretta: The Story of Coretta Scott King* (Minneapolis: Fortress Press, 2006), 101.

7. Mike Feinsilber, "U.S. Snubs King's Goal, Widow Says," *Atlanta Constitution*, June 20, 1968, 1, 12.

8. "Concert Begins King Birth Observance," *Atlanta Constitution*, January 15, 1974, 11A.

9. Ibid.

10. "March, Jobs Rally Recall King's Dream," *Atlanta Constitution*, January 16, 1977, 1A, 4A.

11. "Work a Right, Mays Declares," *Atlanta Constitution*, January 16, 1978, 14A.

12. Houston Bryan Roberson, *Fighting the Good Fight: The Story of the Dexter Avenue King Memorial Baptist Church, 1865–1977* (New York and London: Routledge, 2002), 188.

13. Glenn T. Eskew, "Exploring Civil Rights Heritage Tourism and Historic Preservation as Revitalization Tools in Atlanta" (paper presented at the 2007 Dan Sweat Conference, Georgia State University, Atlanta; revised for publication).

14. William P. Jones, "Working-Class Hero," *The Nation*, January 11, 2006, http://www.thenation.com/doc/20060130/jones/print.

15. Don Wolfensberger, "The Martin Luther King, Jr. Holiday: The Long Struggle in Congress, an Introductory Essay," Woodrow Wilson International Center for Scholars, January 14, 2008, http://www.wilsoncenter.org/events/docs/King%20Holiday-essay-drw.pdf, 3.

16. Ibid.

17. Jimmy Carter, President's Daily Diary, November 5, 1979, and November 6, 1979, http://jimmycarterlibrary.org/documents/diary/1979/d110579t.pdf.

18. Wolfensberger, 7.

19. Michael Eric Dyson, *Why I Love Black Women* (New York: Basic Books, 2003), 76.

Chapter 8

FOUR CHILDREN, ANOTHER LEGACY

In the 15 years after Martin's death, Coretta and Martin's children grew up. The children were a priority of Coretta's, and she continued to work out of the office at her home at 234 Sunset Avenue in Atlanta. However, due to her own schedule of King Center commitments, fundraising, and other engagements, she relied on family members, close friends, and household staff to assist with caring for and transporting the children to school and activities.

About a year after the assassination, Andrew Young suggested to Coretta that she have her children meet with a child psychologist for counseling. He noted that both of the Kennedy families had done this for their children and it would likely be helpful to her children. Coretta determined that the ideal counselor was Lonnie McDonald, who practiced in New York and was a friend of Coretta's from Antioch College. Dr. McDonald visited Atlanta and spent time with each child individually over a few weeks. In his memoir, Dexter King recalled that there were no breakthroughs, but rather the children followed their mother's example "lick your wounds, keep moving, don't question."[1]

As the older children had begun to march with Martin prior to his death, all of the children were involved in commemorative services, fundraisers, and political events. In May 1968, Vice President Hubert Humphrey invited the children to visit the White House, and photographs were taken of him playing with Dexter. Coretta did not restrict such photography, especially if the children were in high-profile settings. As early as 1972, Yolanda and Martin III spoke briefly during the King Day Commemorative Services. These appearances helped the family maintain the love and admiration that the public had had for Martin prior to his death.

Yolanda, Martin, and Dexter had begun school in Spring Street Elementary, an Atlanta Public School, in 1965. In 1969, Yolanda began high school at another public school, Grady High School, from which she graduated, completing a magnet program for drama.

Coretta transferred the other three children to the Galloway School, a small private school that used the open classroom structure to provide for individualized instruction and the development of creativity. The school also included a strong multicultural humanities curriculum that allowed the children to learn about and to appreciate the many cultures of the world.

While Coretta did not restrict the children from appearing in public settings, she was also concerned for their privacy and security, based on the notoriety of the family. Galloway's small size and location in a wealthy neighborhood helped calm Coretta's fears as did the employment of drivers to deliver and pick up the children from school.

In the summers from 1969–1977, the children attended camp for two weeks at Camp Blue Star, a camp owned by the Jewish community in the Blue Ridge Mountains of North Carolina. The Abernathy children also attended, as did the children of Andrew Young. Camp allowed the children the experiences of hiking, sleeping out, and cooking over campfires, experiences that they would not have had in the city.

The children also went on other trips with family friends during holiday vacations and the summer. Sites included the Upper Peninsula of Michigan for snow skiing, where Dexter sprained his ankle, and Lake Tahoe for water skiing.

In his memoir, Dexter recalled occasions when entertainers or other famous people would visit the King household after Martin's death. While in town to do a benefit concert for the SCLC, the Jackson 5 spent time with the King children. Michael, Jermaine, and Tito played games with Martin, Dexter, and Bernice, while Yolanda chatted with Jackie and Randy.

Daddy King assisted Coretta by acting as disciplinarian. Dexter noted that he did not "spare the rod," an attribute that he associated with Daddy King's rural upbringing and physical battles with his own father. As Dexter grew older, he noted that he "was more appreciative of his ethics and the way he took care of business, because he DID take care of business, and you could always count on him if you were in a lurch."[2]

MORE TRAGEDY

The family experienced another tragedy on July 21, 1969, when A. D. King, Martin's younger brother, drowned in a swimming pool in the backyard of his home. The children were in Jamaica at the time, finishing a trip that Uncle A. D. had planned for them. For the second time in less than a year, Coretta and her children participated in a funeral, although this one was much less high profile than that of Martin.

Tragedy struck a third time in 1974, when Alberta King, Martin's mother, was shot by Marcus Wayne Chenault while playing the organ at Ebenezer Baptist Church. A. D.'s son Derek, a seminary student, was in the pulpit, and Daddy King was seated in the front row, as he was preparing to leave town for a speaking engagement. Coretta was not in church, but Dexter was across the street at a store between Sunday School and Morning Worship, and he saw his grandmother wounded and dying.

Upon each of these tragedies, Dexter recalled his mother's admonition at the death of Martin not to hate the killer. "The man who did this was sick. And this is a sick society. But you must learn to forgive. Not to forget but to forgive. You must. Or you will become bitter."[3]

Also in 1974, Coretta received a threat that her children would be kidnapped. This period had seen several other high-profile kidnappings in the United States, from Patty Hearst to the daughter of Atlanta baseball star Hank Aaron. Coretta tightened security around the children, and Atlanta police officers began to pose as teachers at the children's school.

Dexter King remembered that it was difficult to date during his high school years. Some girls (and their parents) were intimidated by the famous connection. Others feared that being in close contact with the Kings would subject them to FBI surveillance or physical harm. Their social lives were kept within a tight network, and none of the children married until after Coretta's death.

CHILDREN OF LEGACY

Ultimately, each of the King children dealt with their lives of tragedy and public attention in a different way. Like others born during the latter days of the post–World War II Baby Boom, they grew up surrounded by television and the media culture. They did not seek out photo opportunities, but they often participated in them in relation to fundraising duties for the King Center or at other commemorative functions.

The children were all influenced by Coretta and her work for peace and social justice. However, they grew up in a different historical era from their parents, and that also affected their views of the world. During the 1970s, African Americans were elected to a variety of local, state, and national political offices. The government and private businesses engaged in affirmative action, which increased employment opportunities. Holdout school districts desegregated and drew area boundaries to promote integrated student bodies. In addition, increasing numbers of groups (from women to the disabled) drew inspiration from the African American civil rights movement and began to seek equality and opportunity within society. All of these factors combined with the influence of Coretta and the Kings to shape the worldviews of their children.

Yolanda followed her parents in going north to attend college. She graduated from Smith College and began a career in drama and motivational speaking in the New York area. A powerful lecturer, Yolanda gave presentations for business, community, and civic groups across the United States and internationally.

She later relocated to California and established Higher Ground Productions. Yolanda's acting roles included portraying Rosa Parks in the NBC television movie *King*, Betty Shabazz in *Death of a Prophet*, and Reena Evers in *Ghosts of Mississippi*.

With Elodia Tate, she developed and published *Open My Eyes, Open My Soul: Celebrating Our Common Humanity*, a collection of poems and stories. The book called readers to overcome racism and strengthen relationships through getting to know each others' stories. Yolanda and Elodia collected the submissions as a result of several competitions and calls for material. They gave out brochures at personal appearances, and they also collected material via a Web site. Submissions came in from across the United States and around the world, from people of all ages, races, and genders. A panel of diverse and experienced editors assisted in evaluating the submissions and identifying the ones for publication. They also awarded one unpublished author a prize, Abby Warmuth for her short story "Danny," about an African American foster child that she played with while growing up in Detroit. Famous contributors to the volume included Maya Angelou, Muhammad Ali, Stevie Wonder, Bernie Siegel, Mattie Stepanek, and Margaret Cho. They organized the submissions into sections by theme, the last of which was "Creating the Beloved Community." The authors' introduction ended with this sentence, "Join us now as we move from the night into the sunlight of acceptance."[4]

A portion of the proceeds from the book went to support the King Center, and another portion went to the Teaching Tolerance program of the Southern Poverty Law Center in Montgomery. Coretta wrote the foreword to the book. She called the anthology "a spiritual travel guide that takes its readers on myriad journeys, deep into the hearts and souls of the wonderful, diverse human beings who populate these pages." She also noted the unity in their stories: "Although the voices in *Open My Eyes, Open My Soul* touch on many facets of the mirror ball of the human experience, together they offer hope that there is an undercurrent of common consciousness that unites all of humanity in some mysterious way, and every effort to promote greater sisterhood and brotherhood, no matter how small or large the scale may be, is worthy of celebration."[5] This expression of unity in diversity echoed Coretta's belief in the holistic nature of life.

Yolanda died of heart failure on May 15, 2007, less than a year after Coretta's death. She was only 50 years old at the time. Her passing was a difficult blow for her siblings, as she had been the main encourager of communication between Dexter (who also lived in California) and Bernice and Martin (who remained in Atlanta).

Martin III graduated from the Galloway School and Morehouse College, his father's alma mater. He was a Fulton County Commissioner from 1987 until 1993. He also followed in his father's footsteps through a tenure as president of the SCLC from 1997–2004. He served on the Board of the King Center, but he did not serve as an executive there until 2004. He lived with his mother at 234 Sunset until shortly before her death. He married Arndrea Waters, a longtime girlfriend, shortly after Coretta's death. She gave birth to Yolanda Renee, the first grandchild of Martin and Coretta's, in 2008.

Dexter transferred from the Galloway School when he went to high school, and he graduated from Frederick Douglass High School, a public school in the neighborhood where his mother lived. Influenced by the 1980s encouragement of independent business and entrepreneurship, he made spending money as a photographer and deejay. He also attended Morehouse College, but he did not graduate. He became close friends with Phillip Jones, who later helped to create Intellectual Properties Management (IPM), a firm that manages the use of Martin's image and words.

Dexter served as president of the King Center two times—first in 1989 (just for a few months) and later from 1994–2004. He continued as chairman of the board after he gave up the presidency.

To pursue an acting career and other business interests in the entertainment arena, Dexter moved to California in 2002. He played the role of Martin in *The Rosa Parks Story* in 2002. He also published his autobiography, *Growing Up King: An Intimate Memoir,* in 2003.

Bernice also graduated from Douglass High School after finishing elementary and middle school at Galloway. She graduated from Spelman College, majoring in psychology.

Bernice has written that as a teenager she became quite depressed and even contemplated suicide. However, in her words, "God saved her," and she pursued that calling by returning to school and earning a Masters of Divinity at the Candler School of Theology of Emory University. She became the only heir of Martin and Coretta's to enter the ministry. In 1996, she published a collection of sermons, *Hard Questions, Heart Answers*. She currently serves as a pastor at New Birth Missionary Baptist Church, a mega-church in DeKalb County. She is also a licensed attorney and member of the Georgia Bar.

During her college years, Bernice was arrested, along with Coretta and Martin III, at an anti-Apartheid protest at the South African Embassy in Washington. Bernice also joined Martin III in continuing to be active with the SCLC. In addition, she has spoken in many venues for the King Center and as a representative of the family at the groundbreaking for the Martin Luther King, Jr. Monument on the National Mall in Washington, D.C.

Bernice cared for Coretta during her final illness and preached the eulogy at her funeral. A year later, she established a scholarship in Coretta's name at Spelman College, using personal funds, funds from the Home Depot, and funds from the New Birth Missionary Baptist Church.

As the children became adults, journalists and other observers began to question the family's handling of Martin's legacy, particularly in terms of the King Estate and Martin's intellectual property. The next few chapters will examine in greater detail the occasions when this issue came up. In the mean time, it is clear that each of the children had different experiences growing up, and those experiences affected their outlook on life and their perceived call to uphold Martin and Coretta's legacy. In addition, some of the apparent inconsistency between the children's views and Martin's views may relate to the fact that Coretta was more realistic and even-handed in her views regarding money and material possessions, whereas Martin gave his income to the movement and also stated on occasions the desire not to own things. The children's adult views are probably not fully in line with either parent, but the parents' views demonstrate the roots from which the children's views emerged.

NOTES

1. Dexter King, *Growing Up King: An Intimate Memoir* (New York: Warner Books, 2003), 62.

2. Ibid., 64.

3. Ibid., 83.

4. Yolanda King and Elodia Tate, eds., *Open My Eyes, Open My Soul: Celebrating Our Common Humanity* (New York: McGraw-Hill, 2004), 22.

5. Coretta Scott King, "Foreword," in *Open My Eyes, Open My Soul*, ed. Yolanda King and Elodia Tate, 13–14 (New York: McGraw-Hill, 2004).

Chapter 9

DIFFICULT TIMES FOR THE KING CENTER

In some ways 1986 was a high point for the work of the King Center. Over the previous 18 years, Coretta had worked tirelessly to establish the Center. She had raised funds to acquire land, to construct buildings, and to set up programs in each of her areas of interest—from the library and archives to institutes on nonviolence. The King Center had a budget of $2 million annually, and there were over 60 people on staff. There were community outreach efforts in early childhood literacy, adult education, and voter education, as well as service for teen parents. A staff member, Ella Mae Brayboy, acted as a one-person referral service for anyone who called or came by requesting help in the name of Martin Luther King, Jr.

In addition, increasing numbers of visitors to Atlanta came to tour the King Center and Martin's birth home. Via these facilities, Atlanta was the first city to take advantage of civil rights sites as venues for cultural heritage tourism.[1] King Center publicity and fundraising materials noted that the site was the "only official international memorial established to continue the legacy and work of Dr. Martin Luther King, Jr."[2]

The year 1986 marked the first celebration of the federal King Holiday, which promised to be another vehicle through which Martin's life could be commemorated and his work continued. Between President Reagan's signing of the bill in 1983 to establish the holiday and the first observance, Coretta worked tirelessly to leverage the impact of the upcoming observance for fundraising for the King Center.

However, there were several problems. The King Center did not have any endowment for the preservation of its facilities. To pay salaries and support programs, as well as to upgrade facilities to make them appeal to tourists, Coretta constantly had to be engaged in fundraising.

THE KING HOLIDAY COMMISSION

Another challenge to Coretta's raising of endowment for the King Center was the structure put in place to implement the celebration and programs of the King Holiday. In 1984, Congress established the Martin Luther King, Jr. Federal Holiday Commission to plan and roll out the new celebration, yet it did not provide any funding or staffing for its operation.

In 1979, Lloyd Davis, a veteran employee of the Department of Housing and Urban Development (HUD), had been detailed via a governmental staffing loan program to provide assistance to the King Center. His original job was to handle community development and housing initiatives for the Center, but he soon took on additional responsibilities including the management of the operations of the Freedom Hall Complex. He arranged for the King Center to be a qualified charity under the Combined Federal Appeal, the U.S. government's equivalent to the United Way. He also facilitated interactions between the Center and the Executive and Legislative Branches during the campaign to establish the King Holiday.

When President Reagan came into office, HUD called for Davis to return to his position in Washington. However, Coretta quickly appealed to President Reagan and Samuel Pierce, the HUD Commissioner (who was African American), to allow for the extension of his work at the King Center. Davis subsequently resigned from the federal government and continued his work at the King Center. He also drafted and saw through Congress the legislation to create the Federal Holiday Commission. In 1984, he became the executive director of the Federal Holiday Commission, although he continued to maintain a title and a variety of duties for the King Center. Coretta was chairman of the Federal King Holiday Commission as well as founder and president of the King Center.

Correspondence from Coretta's files of the Federal King Holiday Commission (housed at the National Archives-SE Region) show her reaching out to allies in city, county, state, and federal government departments seeking grants and contracts to underwrite Center and Commission needs. In 1985, she requested that the Atlanta City Council allocate a portion of the city's hotel/motel tax proceeds, which supported tourist and convention business, to the King Center. (She did not receive the allocation, although the City continued to promote the King site as a tourist attraction.) She also requested $50,000 from Fulton County to provide for maintenance and repairs of the grounds and to purchase a canopy for use in programs. (After deliberation by the Board of Commissioners, they provided the $50,000.) Via the Georgia Department of Industry Tourism and Trade, she requested an annual grant of $200,000. (The State's first funding came via the Georgia Department of Natural Resources providing support for a brochure for the King site, as well as state park system employees who acted as tour guides.)

At the federal level, Coretta reached out to a variety of cabinet secretaries, and she sought to identify opportunities that made sense for both the King Center and the agencies. With the U.S. Department of Commerce, she sought assistance to develop the King Center Gift Shop as a catalogue business. She offered Freedom Hall as a venue for conferences and international delegations. She also indicated that the King Center could provide training in nonviolence and conflict resolution to interested businesses and trade associations. She was a prolific and creative explorer of possibilities. One example was her request to the Department of Commerce to support a lecture series on the theme "The Free Enterprise System: An Agent for Nonviolent Social Change." She also offered the King Center's expertise toward developing foreign trade policies, to prevent economic exploitation, and to eliminate global racism.[3]

From Secretary of State George Shultz and the State Department, Coretta sought support for an international conference on Martin's philosophy and international conflict resolution. She asked Secretary of Housing and Urban Development Samuel Pierce to advocate for a King Center proposal to develop a community partnership model to advance housing and economic development.

Coretta and Lloyd Davis met with White House Chief of Staff Donald Regan on March 14, 1984. In a five-page memo marked "confidential," she laid out the proposed discussion items under the headings, "the contribution which the King Center can make to this administration," "the contribution which this administration can make to the King Center," "the support which the administration can give to the Martin Luther King, Jr. Federal Holiday Commission," and "how the administration should view the King Center." Under the section about the King Center's contributions, she noted that the King Center was nonpolitical and nonpartisan. She also highlighted that the Center retained a close relationship with the administration at the highest levels and that it has received funding via a number of channels under the administration. She included a laundry list of ways in which the administration could provide assistance, ranging from helping to secure a chairman of the Center's capital campaign to raise endowment, to attending the commemorative service on January 20, 1986, to supporting funding via a number of pending applications. She emphasized (as evidenced by the sentence being in all caps) the need to "help the King Center to become firmly established in the public mind, as the only official memorial established to carry on

Dr. king's work and an institution worthy of federal, private, and general public support."[4]

At the end of the memo, in the section about how the administration should view the King Center, she noted they should be "a friend, even though differences on specific issues can be expected." This was Coretta's attempt to cover any conflict that would arise due to differences in political stands of the Administration and the King Center.

In September 1984, Coretta wrote Congressman Peter Rodino, who had been an ally, seeking that he introduce legislation to grant a federal charter to the King Center as "the only official national and international memorial established to continue Martin's legacy and work."[5] She indicated that this protection was needed for the King Center to maintain its position and to prevent "those who would capitalize on Martin's birthday by commercializing the observance" and "those who would use the occasion to advance their own special interests to seize the initiative in this matter."[6] She pointed to the example of the National Academy of Public Administration, which had recently been chartered to improve governmental operations. This bill did not go forward.

THE KING CENTER'S MULTIPLE MISSIONS: COMMEMORATION AND ACTIVISM

If all of these fundraising proposals and grant applications had been funded, it would have been very difficult for the King Center, even with a staff of 60, to implement all of the programs and activities they were offering to carry out. In addition, some observers, such as Frederick Allen, the political editor for the *Atlanta Constitution,* began to question "can we memorialize King while calling for change?"[7]

Allen pointed out the contrast between Coretta's role as widow and keeper of Martin's history vis-à-vis one who was involved in contemporary political and social action. In 1984, she had publicly endorsed Walter Mondale over Ronald Reagan. Ironically, it was President Reagan who had signed the bill to establish King Day as a federal holiday.

The Reagan Administration put an emphasis on increasing military spending and building up America's defense infrastructure, after what they saw as the neglect of such during the Carter administration. In the 1985 "State of the Dream" lecture, Coretta called, "Let us revive the nonviolent revolution. It will require that we question established values, that we question the strange and frightening vision that says we must spend millions on Star Wars weapons."[8] Star Wars was an initiative of the Reagan administration that would develop a missile defense system.

The King Center also hosted activists, even at the commemorative church services, who spoke out against U.S. violence around the world and took sides in international political disputes. As Frederick Allen pointed out, "A good many of the corporate sponsors who wish to honor Dr. King obviously prefer the sanctity of his memory to the idea of underwriting what his politics might be today."[9]

In addition, there was a difference of opinion about how much work was left to do to fulfill Martin's vision. Clarence Pendleton, the chairman of the U.S. Civil Rights Commission, appointed by President Reagan, suggested, "I'm certain that the dream has already been satisfied. I think the dream gets confused with the memory."[10]

However, Coretta also resented it if a person referred to her as only the widow of Martin Luther King, Jr. She saw Martin's leadership and philosophy as significant to more than the civil rights arena, and this was the justification behind the variety of topics that she sought for the King Center to address. "Martin always spoke to collective evils in the world. He was holistic in his philosophy. If you don't understand that about Martin, you're missing it."[11] Coretta was quite clear that she was the primary interpreter and promoter of Martin's teachings and ongoing legacy. Because she felt that she, too, was holistic, and because she had faith in the rightness of her causes, she assumed that things would work out and that politics would not get in the way of her good efforts. As debate in government and the public square was becoming more partisan and divided, this was a somewhat naïve position.

1986 HOLIDAY

The Atlanta Chamber of Commerce and the State of Georgia stepped in to assist with the planning of the January 1986 events in Atlanta in November of 1985. The Federal Holiday Commission, which was supposed to be overseeing the planning, had little money and few staff. While the timeline was short and the obstacle of raising funds was ahead, Atlanta's leadership did not want to allow this observance in honor of their native son to fail.

These business community volunteers knew that they would need to turn over their plans to Coretta and to Andrew Young (who was then Mayor of Atlanta). As an example of the logistical and philosophical challenges, planners invited all branches of the military to march in the parade in Atlanta, but they requested that soldiers not carry weapons, so as not to contradict Martin's pacifist philosophy. Ultimately, Coretta did compromise somewhat on her position, and she allowed the military color guard units to carry rifles, as that is their tradition. She also agreed that law-enforcement personnel could carry weapons for self-defense as they handled crowd control.[12]

After a scramble, the 1986 birthday observances went off as planned. President Reagan spoke at Martin Luther King, Jr. Elementary School in Washington, D.C. and recounted the struggles of the Civil Rights era.

> Our country is different because Martin Luther King, Jr. made it better by the way he lived his life. America had a conscience . . . It wouldn't let us hide from the truth and it wouldn't let us sleep until we all, together, as a whole country, admitted that all people are equal and that in America there should be no second-class citizens. Our national conscience told us to change and start to be fair.[13]

President Reagan, like his cabinet official, felt that America had changed as a result of Martin's work. Equality of opportunity was now available, and there was no longer a need for racial preferences or affirmative action.

The same day as President Reagan's speech, Jesse Jackson spoke at Ebenezer Baptist in Atlanta and "accused President Reagan and the media of contributing to a distorted image of King's legacy. King was not a non-threatening dreamer. His mission was to disturb the comfortable and comfort the disturbed."[14] Coretta was not in attendance for either speech, but the contrast indicates the beginning of what would be a long battle over the definition of Martin's legacy. Some representatives of business and political interests sought to praise Martin for all that he did in the past. They implied that through his work, segregation had been ended, voting rights had been achieved, and freedom and opportunity had been opened to all. This notion conflicted with Coretta's view, which intended to apply Martin's principles to ongoing national and international challenges.

A third *Atlanta Constitution* article from January 16, 1986, highlighted Coretta's own work style and emphasis. Howard Pousner described Coretta's preparations for an interview on C-SPAN. As the interviewer attempted to lay out a plan for their discussion, "Ms. King decided to lay out her own agenda. 'Let me tell you,' she interrupted, 'I can't just talk about the holiday, because it's only one part of what I'm doing through my work at the Martin Luther King Center for Nonviolent Social Change in Atlanta.'" Pousner continued, noting that Coretta's bluntness has given her a reputation as overbearing among some people. However, her forceful personality was also the key to her success. "Often appearing to be an army of one, she has never stopped marching."[15]

CORETTA'S WORK STYLE

During this period, Coretta worked exhaustive days, up to 18 hours. When she traveled, she constantly looked for a pay phone to call the Center and check in. She flew first class, which she felt was necessary for security. An assistant traveled with her, and she had a driver. Once her children were grown, she worked out of an office in the King Center, which she filled with awards and photographs of herself with entertainers and political leaders.

Her position at the King Center was called founder and president. She did not draw a salary, supporting herself through speeches and royalties from her and Martin's writings. She also sought to maintain tight leadership of the Center because "You can't build anything that's worthwhile unless you personally get involved. You can't hire folks to do your work for you . . . because there's not enough dedication out there anywhere. You can't buy it. It has to be born."[16]

While the King Center did have 60 staff members, Coretta exercised tight control of the facility, occasionally down to the level of determining how many legal pads to purchase for the offices. She also relied greatly on Christine Farris, Martin's sister, who served as treasurer for the King Center, and she entrusted Isaac Farris, Christine's husband, to handle licensing agreements involving Martin's image.

The King Center obtained a reputation for not starting meetings on time and for keeping visitors and reporters waiting a long time for scheduled interviews. Some observers noted that it followed the flavor and casual style of some of the civil rights movements' organizations. They attested that style to the involvement of community people and volunteers. But as the Center moved from being the founder's dream to an established nonprofit organization, others looked for them to implement more efficient business practices.

In 1986, two Atlanta-based consulting groups stepped in to provide free services. The Atlanta Chamber of Commerce and Central Atlanta Progress also gave suggestions and facilitated fundraising efforts.

The Center hired an experienced chief operating officer as well as a development director. But they also experienced regular turnover, as executives found that all decisions, of whatever magnitude, still needed to run through Coretta and the board.

In 1987, the Federal King Holiday Commission reported that it continued to struggle. Lloyd Davis continued to wear dual hats. He had to use borrowed office space in Washington and he relied on donated time from other federal agencies to handle mailings and publicity for the Holiday. The King Center Board had to forgive the Commission for $60,000 in operating costs that they had handled on behalf of the Commission. In addition, the King Center had to donate $25,000 cash to maintain the operations of the Commission. The Commission continued to seek additional funding through governmental sources. When its charter was extended in 1989, it did receive a $300,000 annual appropriation. However, this did not resolve the funding struggles for the King Center.

In 1988, the Atlanta media reported that Fulton County Sheriff Richard Lankford was assigning a deputy to the King Center full time to provide security for the family. The reports filed by this deputy included embarrassing details such as the fact that he had been dispatched to oversee the towing of a disabled car for Martin Luther King III (who was almost 30 years old at the time). An editorial in the *Atlanta Constitution* suggested that the King family, as private citizens, should take responsibility for their own security. Fulton County discontinued providing the deputy, and the King Center's private force took on the tasks at hand. Two years later, Coretta testified as a character witness in the federal trial of Sheriff Lankford who was accused of extortion and tax evasion.

PASSING THE TORCH AND TAKING IT BACK

Coretta resigned as president of the King Center in January 1989, in conjunction with the 20th commemorative service. She was 62 years old. Her replacement was her son Dexter, who was 27 at the time. Coretta retained the title of CEO, while Dexter became president. Dexter had been working at the Center for a couple of years and held the title of director of special events prior to his promotion. In announcing the change, Coretta stated that her plan was to focus on promoting the center's message nationally and internationally and on raising endowment funds, while allowing him to manage day-to-day operations. Dexter highlighted that his area of interest was in mobilizing "the younger generation, ages 18 to 40, for a nonviolent army, making the center the 'West Point' of nonviolence . . . I hope to reach out to a new generation of soldiers of the post-civil rights era . . . people like myself who were just children when the movement began."[17]

About six months later, Dexter resigned. Board members reported that Dexter's resignation was the result of a misunderstanding. It was their expectation that when Dexter was hired, he would serve a period of training, in which he would continue to report to Coretta and them. Dexter bristled and ultimately rejected this arrangement of a title without authority. In his memoir, Dexter recounted that he and Coretta "had a verbal knock-down-drag-out argument" about the situation. He compared it to the verbal spars that Martin had with Daddy King, as well as the physical ones that Daddy King had had with his father.[18] The situation hurt Dexter, but he, Coretta, and the board determined that it was better to move on. Dexter remained a member of the King Center Board, and Coretta resumed the position of president and CEO.

In 1991, the King Center hired Dr. Ronald Quincy as executive director, a new title for the Center. His previous position was associate vice president and assistant to the president at Harvard University. The Reverend Joseph Lowery, a board member, said "we are trying to bring in an able administrator to free up Mrs. King to be a spokesperson and symbol."[19]

During Quincy's three-year tenure, corporate donations to the King Center increased. However, Quincy resigned in March 1994. He did not cite specific reasons for his departure, but the Atlanta media speculated that it marked continued resistance to leadership from outside the family. In addition, it appeared that Coretta was not comfortable turning administrative decisions over to others. As she had asserted in an interview in the *Atlanta Constitution* in 1993, she was not comfortable with the role of symbol; she wanted to lead.

In October 1994, the King Center announced that Dexter King would become CEO again, as well as chairman of the board, effective March 1995. Coretta would remain as a board member.

DEXTER'S LEADERSHIP, ROUND TWO

An early priority for development during Dexter's second term was an interactive museum that would be controlled by the Center. Dexter wanted to place this museum on the same land where the National Park Service intended to build an upgraded visitors' center prior to the 1996 Atlanta Olympic Games. The proposed King family museum would be fee-based, whereas the National Park Service center would be free.

In December 1994, Coretta held an emotional press conference in which she stated that "the same evil forces that destroyed Martin Luther King are now trying to destroy my family."[20] Dexter indicated that the National Park Service had reneged on an agreement to allow the King Center to develop exhibits about Martin in the new visitors' center. Dexter also spoke and accused the *Atlanta Journal-Constitution* of "assassinating their character" by implying they would reap material profit from the proposed museum. Coretta echoed that her motives and those of her children had never been about personal enrichment.

Soon after this, the family also ordered the National Park Service to stop offering tours of the Birth Home. Representative John Lewis, a civil rights veteran who had advocated for federal funding for upgrading the site, began to attempt to mediate between the sides. National Park Service spokespeople also indicated that they saw their work as complementary to the King efforts, rather than competitive.

During the dispute, the Park Service put on hold plans to develop an exhibit for the new visitors' center about Coretta and her role in extending Martin's legacy. Dexter was also critical of the plans for an exhibit on Martin, saying that they were "static."

In December 1994, Dexter told the media that he was in negotiations with Oppenheimer and Company regarding funding for the interactive museum. It would be its own nonprofit, he indicated. Oppenheimer noted that the investment would require municipal bonds in order to generate tax incentives for investors. The King Family also placed an ad in the *Atlanta Journal Constitution* indicating that profits from the museum would be used for housing for the homeless and various community programs.

On January 16, 1995, Dexter was installed as leader of the King Center during the commemorative service for Martin. In his speech, he noted a contrast between the goals of the generations: "My father delivered to his generation political freedom. I would like to deliver to my generation economic freedom."[21] However, funding for the interactive museum never came together, and by April of 1995, the two sides came to a truce, with Dexter calling the National Park Service "a partner in promoting his father's legacy."[22]

Coretta also made a farewell speech during the 1995 commemorative service, after a passionate introduction by Andrew Young. She indicated that she would continue to serve as an advisor to the Center as well as a fundraiser. She also intended to write another memoir about her life after Martin's death. "I don't want you to think I'll be sitting home watching the world go by," she said.[23]

NOTES

1. Glenn T. Eskew, "Exploring Civil Rights Heritage Tourism and Historic Preservation as Revitalization Tools in Atlanta" (paper presented at the 2007 Dan Sweat Conference, Georgia State University, Atlanta; revised for publication).

2. Memo, "Possible Areas for Collaboration," included in letter to Malcolm Baldridge, Secretary, U.S. Department of Commerce, March 26, 1984; Coretta

Scott King Correspondence File, Papers of the Martin Luther King, Jr. Federal Holiday Commission, National Archives–SE Region, Morrow, Georgia, 1.

3. Ibid., 1–2.

4. Memo, "Meeting with White House Chief of Staff, Donald Regan," March 14, 1984; Coretta Scott King Correspondence File, Papers of the Martin Luther King Jr. Federal Holiday Commission, National Archives–SE Region, Morrow, Georgia, 2.

5. Coretta Scott King letter to Congressman Peter W. Rodino, September 7, 1984; Coretta Scott King Correspondence File, Papers of the Martin Luther King Jr. Federal Holiday Commission, National Archives–SE Region, Morrow, Georgia, 1.

6. Ibid.

7. Frederick Allen, "Can We Memorialize King While Calling for Change?" *Atlanta Constitution*, November 21, 1985, A2.

8. Bill Montgomery, "Mrs. King Pins Famine Blame: Philosophy of Late Husband Urged to Help Battle World Hunger," *Atlanta Constitution*, January 12, 1985, C14.

9. Allen, "Can We Memorialize King."

10. Priscilla Painton, "King Center Struggles to Meet Social Needs, Be a Memorial," *Atlanta Constitution*, January 17, 1986, 1A, 12A.

11. Howard Pousner, "Coretta King Married the Man and His Vision," *Atlanta Constitution*, January 16, 1986, 1A, 8A.

12. Jane O. Hansen, "Chamber to Help out with King Holiday Planning," *Atlanta Constitution*, November 7, 1985.

13. Bob Dart, "Reagan Marks King's Birthday," *Atlanta Constitution*, January 16, 1986, 1A, 7A.

14. Priscilla Painton, "Follow King by Helping the Poor, Jesse Jackson Urges Audience," *Atlanta Constitution*, January 16, 1986, 7A.

15. Howard Pousner, "Coretta King Married," 1A.

16. Ibid., 8A.

17. Derrick Hiamon, "Mrs. King Resigns Post at Center," *Atlanta Constitution*, January 15, 1989, 1A, 16A.

18. Dexter King, *Growing Up King: An Intimate Memoir* (New York: Warner Books, 2003), 168.

19. Gary Pomerantz, "Harvard Administrator to Join King Center," *Atlanta Constitution*, July 3, 1991, D1, D7.

20. John Blake, "Family Cites 'Evil Forces' at Work," *Atlanta Constitution*, December 23, 1994, E1.

21. John Blake, "King Center Torch Passed," *Atlanta Constitution*, January 17, 1995, B9.

22. John Blake, "King Center, Federal Agency Settle Dispute," *Atlanta Constitution*, April 2, 1995, A1.

23. Ibid.

The Scott family home in Perry County, Alabama, built by Obediah Scott adjacent to his grocery store, as it appears today. Coretta Scott and Martin Luther King, Jr., were married on the porch of this house on June 18, 1953. (Photograph courtesy of Laura T. McCarty).

On March 22, 1956, Rev. Ralph Abernathy (left) greets Rev. Martin Luther King, Jr., at the courthouse in Montgomery, where King had just been found guilty of leading the Montgomery bus boycott. King's fine was suspended pending an appeal. A jubilant Coretta stands to her husband's right. (AP Photo/Gene Herrick).

The Kings, both wearing garlands brought by enthusiastic supporters, arrive at the airport in New Delhi on Feb. 10, 1959, for, in Martin's words, a "four-week pilgrimage in India, which to me means Mahatma Gandhi." (AP Photo/R. Satakopan).

In early February 1965, Coretta Scott King and Juanita Abernathy, accompanied by Rev. Fred Shuttlesworth, unsuccessfully attempt to visit their spouses at the Selma, Alabama, jail. Martin Luther King, Jr., and Ralph Abernathy had been imprisoned for leading voter registration demonstrations. (AP Photo).

Dr. Martin Luther King, Jr., and Coretta Scott King, with Rev. F. D. Reese, of Selma (to Coretta's left), lead thousands of civil rights demonstrators in the final day of the March 21–March 25, 1965, voting rights march from Selma to the state capitol at Montgomery. Two previous march attempts had been violently turned back at the Edmund Pettus Bridge in Selma; the third succeeded because of the presence of federal troops ordered in by Pres. Lyndon B. Johnson. (AP Photo).

Coretta Scott King at an October 1965 news conference in Trenton, New Jersey, where she is about to perform at a Freedom Concert. (AP Photo).

Coretta Scott King and her children Martin Luther III, age 10, Dexter, age 7, and Yolanda, age 12, follow the casket of Dr. Martin Luther King, Jr., into an Atlanta funeral home on April 5, 1968. With them is Alberta Williams King, Martin's mother. Among the other mourners are (left) Martin's brother, the Rev. A. D. Williams King, and Dr. Ralph Abernathy. (AP Photo/Bill Hudson).

Coretta Scott King speaks about her intention to carry on her husband's work during a news conference on April 6, 1968. With her is Ralph Abernathy, who succeeded Martin Luther King, Jr., as head of the Southern Christian Leadership Conference. (AP Photo/Charles E. Knoblock).

Pres. Jimmy Carter and Rosalynn Carter join Martin Luther King, Sr., Andrew Young, Coretta Scott King, and other civil rights leaders at the Ebenezer Baptist Church in Atlanta on the eve of Martin Luther King, Jr.'s birthday in 1979. (Courtesy: Jimmy Carter Library/183007).

Pres. Ronald Reagan signs the bill establishing Martin Luther King, Jr.'s birthday as a federal holiday, as Coretta Scott King looks on. Also present at the Nov. 2, 1983, ceremony in Washington, D.C., are Vice President George H. W. Bush (left), Republican senators Charles McCurdy Mathias and Bob Dole, and representatives Jack Kemp (R-N.Y.) and Katie Hall (D-Ind.). (AP Photo/Barry Thumma).

Protesting against apartheid in South Africa, Coretta Scott King walks a picket line at the South African Embassy in Washington, D.C., in November 1984. (AP Photo/ Charles Tasnadi).

In June 1990, Nelson Mandela becomes the first recipient of the Martin Luther King Jr. International Freedom Award. With Mandela and Coretta Scott King at the award ceremony at the Big Bethel African Methodist Episcopal church in Atlanta is Mandela's wife Winnie. (AP Photo/David Longstreath).

Coretta Scott King delivers a keynote speech at the March 2000 United Jewish Communities Young Leadership Conference in Washington, D.C. (AP Photo/Joe Marquette).

Monument honoring Coretta at the Mount Tabor AME-Zion Church in Perry County, Alabama, erected by the SCLC/Women's Organizational Movement for Equality Now, Inc. (Photograph courtesy of Laura T. McCarty).

Chapter 10

CORETTA ON THE INTERNATIONAL STAGE

Both the U.S. civil rights movement and the end of colonialism in Africa and Asia occurred after World War II. African American veterans returned to the American South determined to overthrow Jim Crow, having seen the horrors of extreme racial ideology in Europe and the Pacific. In addition, some veterans had traveled to countries that were about to emerge from colonialism and thus gained a better sense of the connectedness of people of color around the world.

Political agreements such as the 1941 Atlantic Charter proposed that the United States and Great Britain would no longer seek control over foreign territories. In addition, it asserted that people had a right to self-determination and that current territorial control should be modified if the people of those areas requested it. These principles gave hope to the movements for independence underway in countries such as India and Indochina. After the end of World War II, the former colonial powers were weakened because they had had to devote much money and people to fighting the war. They no longer had the funds and mechanisms to maintain control of territories far removed from their home base.

In 1955, representatives of 29 countries from Asia, the Middle East, and Africa gathered in Bandung, Indonesia, for a conference. The Indonesian president gave a speech calling for the birth of new countries in Asia and Africa. The conference also advocated economic and social cooperation between the new countries, under the auspices of the United Nations, rather than under alignment with either the United States or the Soviet Union. At the time, Asian countries were further along in becoming independent than African ones were, but Asia also was dealing with issues that emerged from whether China would assert colonial authority over countries in its area.

African American political, educational, and religious leaders began to pay greater attention to the developments in these new nations, particularly those in Africa. Martin and Coretta visited Ghana in 1957 as part of a delegation of African American leaders to witness the inauguration of its national government, the first to develop out of colonialism.

Another development that assisted in this increased awareness of these geopolitical actions was the rise of the mass media and television. The first communications satellite, Telstar I, was launched in 1962, and it provided for television pictures to be shown across the Atlantic. People in Europe and in the urban areas of Africa and Asia were able to see images of the American civil rights struggle and to hear Martin's speeches. Likewise, Americans could see and learn about the leaders and cultures of new postcolonial African states.

SOUTH AFRICA

South Africa was a country whose racial struggles particularly captured the interest of African Americans because they saw some parallels to their own situation. Dutch Colonists established communities at the southern tip of Africa in the seventeenth century. They pushed aside native Africans and took their land. Over the next 250 years, Europeans continued to dominate the region. In the early twentieth century, workers came into the region from India to work in mines, farms, and factories. They were also discriminated against, as were Africans and Coloureds (people of mixed ancestry). Since the arrival of the Europeans, the South African society practiced segregation.

In 1948, the National Party won an election and took over the South African government. It instituted a policy called *apartheid* (from the Afrikaans word for "separation"). Under this practice, the government classified each person according to a racial category, and they made sure that the different categories lived apart from each other as much as possible. They set up Bantu Homelands in which the Africans were to live. The rest of the country, including the major cities, ports, industrial areas, and prime farm land, was reserved for persons of European descent (who only made up 20% of the population).

Soon after the establishment of apartheid, a practical flaw in the system emerged. Factories, agricultural businesses, and mines relied on African and Coloured laborers to function. Europeans also hired African domestic workers, and merchants marketed goods to African buyers. The Bantu

Homelands did not develop effective economies, and Africans migrated to the cities to live and work.

The next step of the apartheid regime was to regulate the comings and goings of Africans within the country. They could work, but they had to maintain passes to document their identity and permission to travel. They were restricted to living in townships on the outskirts of the urban areas, and they had to return to those areas by certain times of day. Soweto, an abbreviation for Southwest Township, became a major population center for Africans around Johannesburg. The state also set up strict laws for restaurants, entertainment venues, and transportation systems, designed to prevent interactions between the Africans and the Europeans, and they outlawed interracial marriages and forbid integration at churches. They set up separate schools, whose curricula reinforced to the African students that they were not equal to Europeans.

Just as resistance to injustice emerged out of segregation in the United States, resistance began in South Africa. Prior to the establishment of apartheid, Gandhi had been part of an Indian resistance movement in South Africa during the first decade of the twentieth century. He tested and implemented some of his tactics of nonviolence that later were crucial to his success in the Quit India movement.

After the establishment of apartheid, various resistance groups began to act. One of the most significant was the African National Congress (ANC), which mounted a nonviolent Defiance Campaign in 1953. On multiple occasions, the South African government retaliated strongly against the protestors, including whippings, arrests, and killings. During a protest in Sharpeville, police killed 69 and wounded 180. This massacre caused Nelson Mandela, one of the leaders of the ANC, to reject nonviolence, quoting a proverb that *the attacks of the wild beast cannot be averted with only bare hands.* Thus, the ANC began to use sabotage and other acts of violence to present their case against apartheid. In 1964, Nelson Mandela was arrested and taken to prison for what would be an almost 30-year stay.

In 1965, Martin made a speech at Hunter College in New York City, in which he aligned the American civil rights struggle with those ongoing in Africa. He noted that Africa is the land of origin for the ancestors of most African Americans. He also acknowledged that he drew inspiration from some of the African liberation movements as he developed the tactics of the civil rights movement. In addition, he stated that the struggle for freedom is not limited by geographic boundaries; it is universal. "Injustice anywhere is injustice everywhere, for we are tied together in a garment of mutuality. What happens in Johannesburg affects Birmingham, however indirectly. Our heritage is in Africa. We should never seek to break the ties, nor should the Africans."[1]

Martin never visited South Africa. He was invited in 1966, but he was not able to get a visa. However, Coretta maintained interest in and connections to Africa as she developed the King Center. As the worldwide anti-apartheid movement increased in the 1970s and '80s, she played a significant role, working with the American Congressional Black Caucus and other groups.

The International Olympic Committee prohibited South Africa from participating in 1964 and 1968 due to objections to apartheid. Jackie Robinson, the American groundbreaking baseball player, led the effort in 1968 to ensure that they not be allowed to participate.

Another tactic was economic disengagement or divestment. Shortly before his death, Martin suggested that American companies cease investment in South Africa. Two early targets were the Chase Manhattan Bank and CitiBank (then called the National City Bank of New York). When South African Airlines began direct flights to the United States to promote tourism, African American groups purchased newspaper ads stating that tourism in South Africa was racist. In 1970, African American employees at Polaroid protested their company's business dealings in South Africa and suggested that Polaroid photographs were being used to develop apartheid passes and permits. At first the company denied those charges, but in 1977, when a clear connection was documented in the American media, the company left South Africa.

Nonprofit groups, such as the King Center, and educational institutions, including historically black colleges, struggled with the issue of how to divest from South Africa. Because of the rise of the global economy, with international investments as a common practice, it was not easy to identify all of the ways that an organization was connected to South Africa. Once investment connections were confirmed, another dilemma was figuring out the ways in which divestment would impact on the Africans who were employed by mines and industries. Groups in the United States debated as to what the correct tactics were to bring down apartheid, just as they had debated about tactics in the civil rights movement.

In the late 1970s, African American organizations collaborated to form TransAfrica, a lobbying group. They began to organize mass protests at the South African Embassy in Washington, D.C. They timed their protests between March 21 (the date of the Sharpeville Massacre) and April 4 (the date of Martin's assassination), calling them "Days of Action Against Apartheid."

On August 12, 1985, Coretta participated in a march and protest in Washington, D.C. Other dignitaries involved included actors Paul Newman and Tony Randall, singer Harry Belafonte, Mayor Ed Koch of New York, Georgia State Senator Julian Bond, and the Reverend Jesse Jackson. Judy Goldsmith, president of the National Association for Women; Benjamin Hooks, director of the NAACP; and Walter Fauntroy, Washington, D.C. Delegate to Congress, also took part. A main speaker was the Reverend Leon Sullivan, a pastor from Philadelphia, whose set of "Sullivan Principles" offered guidelines for American businesses in dealing with entities in South Africa. At the rally, organizers declared the day a "day of mourning for Blacks in South Africa." The march also took on the style of a mock funeral.

Coretta spoke, proclaiming that "Apartheid is beginning to crumble. What it will be replaced by depends on actions in this country and in other nations." She also incorporated some of Martin's words: "Injustice anywhere is a threat to justice everywhere," when noting the need to protest in the United States about an issue that was occurring in a country far away.[2]

The following day, Coretta, Yolanda, Martin III, and Bernice were arrested during a protest at the South African Embassy in Washington, D.C. Following in Martin's footsteps, they went to jail, although they were released after a couple of hours.

In September 1986, Coretta traveled to South Africa accompanied by a group of King Center board members. She had plans to meet with a variety of leaders, representing multiple views on the conflict, including President P. W. Botha, Zulu Chief Gatsha Buthelezi, Winnie Mandela of the African National Congress, and Allan Boesak of the United Democratic Front. She saw herself as a mediator, engaged in promoting dialogue. She had been briefed by the U.S. government and by American African American leaders that meetings with South African government leaders might preclude her ability to meet with anti-apartheid leaders. However, "they said that they felt if anyone could get an audience with all of them I would probably be able to do that because of what I represent and the symbolism of Martin Luther King."[3] Still, when she reached South Africa, the anti-apartheid forces made it clear that they would not meet with her if she met with Botha or Buthelezi. The trip coincided with a date that the government intended to hang three ANC members, and it also came shortly after the government razing of a squatters' camp, about which there was great public outrage in the black community. Ultimately, Coretta called off the meetings with Botha and Buthelezi, indicating in a statement to the press that they were postponed. She did meet with Winnie Mandela.

The trip was a public relations nightmare in South Africa and the United States. Newspapers criticized Coretta for staying in exclusive hotels that were not affordable for South Africans. They also suggested that it was wrong for her to be guarded by South African security forces. They questioned why she also called off a tour of Soweto, the country's largest black township. On the other hand, newspapers loyal to the South African government suggested that Coretta had let herself be intimidated into abandoning a chance for dialogue due to unreasonable demands from ANC leaders.

In the end, Coretta admitted that "South African politics had proven more complex than I'd originally thought."[4] Advisors on the trip gave her varying responses as they talked and prayed about what to do. However, a phone call to Andrew Young, who was back in the United States, ultimately assured her that it was best that she align herself solidly with the anti-apartheid forces, which connected better with her own base of African American support.

After the trip, she met with President Reagan and Secretary of State George Shultz and claimed that the trip was a success. "The nonviolent process was working through all of this. We took the high road."[5] She also encouraged President Reagan to enact economic sanctions against South Africa. This was not in line with President Reagan's beliefs, as he attempted to work for change through engagement with the South African government.

Coretta and the King Center continued to remain anti-apartheid, as well as to offer nonviolence as a model for resolving the conflict in South Africa. In the face of extreme government violence and oppression, the South Africans did not adopt nonviolence, but the increased international scrutiny and economic pressure caused the government to be more peaceful in dealing with the ANC, which enabled the ANC to negotiate and work toward a resolution to the conflict.

The King Center, like many other nonprofits of that era, faced a dilemma regarding accepting funding from corporations who were involved in South Africa. Some activists continued to call for divestment in order to isolate the South African government economically. But the King Center did not pursue such a policy. Coretta noted, "We approach corporations nonviolently with our programs and we say we spend money with you and we expect you to recognize our principles."[6] Whether the corporations that funded the King Center were ever fully in line with their principles is debatable.

But in spite of the challenges, Coretta continued to build her alliance with Winnie and Nelson Mandela, as well as Archbishop Desmond Tutu. After his release from prison in 1990, Nelson Mandela visited Atlanta during a national fundraising tour. He attracted 54,000 people to a program at Georgia Tech's Bobby Dodd Stadium. Some young attendees in the crowd noted that, for their generation, the event compared to the experience of their parents in hearing Martin speak.

Prior to the public rally, Nelson Mandela stopped at the King Center and had a private meeting with Coretta. Winnie Mandela returned to Atlanta to be the grand marshal of the King Holiday march in 1992. During another fundraising trip in July 1993, Nelson laid another wreath at Martin's grave and visited with Coretta. In 1996, Coretta attended the inauguration of Nelson as President of South Africa.

CORETTA AS PEACE ACTIVIST

Besides South Africa, Coretta participated in other international efforts throughout the 1970s and 1980s. In 1970, Mrs. Naida King Okaye, who was of Biafran descent, flew to Atlanta and requested a meeting with Coretta to express her concerns about turmoil in Nigeria. Speaking of Coretta, she suggested, "She's such a world-wide figure. She has no ax to grind. Maybe Gowon [the leader of Nigeria] will listen to her. No one else has been able to get through."[7] A King Center representative had suggested that Mrs. Okaye travel to Atlanta and seek an appointment, after she had previously tried to appeal to President Richard Nixon but got no further than a secretary. Coretta was not able to change the situation in Nigeria substantially, but the media coverage of Mrs. Okaye's request added to the image of Coretta as a player on the international stage.

When Jomo Kenyatta, the President of Kenya, died in 1978, President Jimmy Carter asked Coretta to represent the United States at the state funeral. President Carter maintained close ties to both Coretta and Daddy King, and these helped him remain in a positive light among African American political and business leaders.

Coretta sent a telegram to President Carter on April 6, 1978, congratulating him for his decision to scrap plans for the neutron bomb. He had announced his decision on April 4, and Coretta noted this as a sign of support for nonviolence. "I write aware of pressures upon you, hoping you can make nonviolence a shining reality in this century."[8] President Carter wrote her back the next day, noting that he was moved by her telegram.

Coretta joined Margaret Papandreou, the U.S.–born wife of the Greek Prime Minister, on a "peace cruise" of the Mediterranean in 1988, prior to a summit between President Reagan and Soviet leader Gorbachev in April 1988. Women from other peace organizations across the United States and Europe participated in the cruise, which called for the summit to include discussion of peace and disarmament issues. Coretta had been involved with organizations working toward disarmament since the late 1950s.

In the late 1980s, the Cold War between the United States and the Soviet Union ended. The USSR loosened their control over countries in Eastern Europe, allowing them to form independent governments. A final sign of this change was the tearing down of the Berlin Wall that separated Germany into two countries.

With the end of the Cold War, Coretta called for reallocations in the budgetary priorities of the United States. In particular, she asked that military spending be redirected to support education and social welfare activities. In spring 1990, she published a column in the journal *Social Policy* that described the changes she wanted to see. "What is at stake in the upcoming budget debate is not only the welfare of impoverished and needy American citizens, who have been neglected for so long, but the economic strength of the nation and our competitive position in the world market."[9]

Coretta also spoke out about issues in the Middle East. In 1988, she called for Israel to release a Palestinian activist, Mubarek Awad. Awad was an alumnus of a nonviolence institute at the King Center, and Coretta pronounced him an adept follower of "Kingian nonviolence."[10]

In 1990, Iraq invaded Kuwait. The U.S. government and allied nations expressed concern at this aggression, and the UN Security Council passed a resolution that authorized use of force against Iraq if they did not leave Kuwait by January 15, 1991. In December 1990, Coretta noted the irony of this date (Martin's birthday). With SCLC President Joseph Lowery, she announced, "We will not tolerate making this a day of war and military aggression." In addition, they noted that they were concerned as to what would come as the result of an American invasion to expel the Iraqis: "We are convinced that United States military action would create more problems than it can resolve."[11]

Iraq did not leave Kuwait, and the United States and a coalition of allies launched a military effort to remove them on January 16, 1991. This placed the beginning of the operation during the King Holiday commemoration. Colin Powell, who was Chairman of the Joint Chiefs of Staff, had been scheduled to serve as a Grand Marshall for the parade, but he withdrew in December as tensions grew in the Middle East. On the other hand, 3,000 Atlanta area students participated in workshops on nonviolence and opposition to racism.

Coretta spoke out against the war on several occasions. At the opening of King Week, she reiterated that "any war in Kuwait would be wrong. The followers of Martin Luther King, Jr. should protest against it with the same fervor that brought an end to the Vietnam War."[12] Several hundred protestors gathered at Martin's tomb on January 15, 1991, to express their opposition to the war.

Once the war began, Coretta called for a cease fire. During the 1991 State of the Dream address, she praised Israel for not retaliating after experiencing two missile attacks from Iraq. She also criticized governmental funding priorities, noting that out of every dollar collected in federal taxes, $.55 went to the military whereas only $.02 went to education. At the Commemorative Service, Andrew Young and Maynard Jackson echoed Coretta's opposition to the war and emphasized the significance of the patriotism and commitment of African Americans in the military.

The Persian Gulf War ended in February 1991, after Iraqi forces retreated from Kuwait. President George H. W. Bush determined not to pursue them into Baghdad. At this point, Coretta and Joseph Lowery combined efforts to call for an international conference to deal with Middle East problems, including the withdrawal of U.S. troops and the reduction of American dependence on foreign oil.

Ten years later, on September 11, 2001, terrorists hijacked airplanes and attacked the World Trade Center in New York City as well as the Pentagon on the outskirts of Washington, D.C. A third plane crashed in Pennsylvania after passengers subdued the hijackers and prevented another planned attack on Washington. In response to this international tragedy, Coretta noted, "As we mourn for the victims of this vicious atrocity, we must not yield to the temptation to let the perpetrators drag us down into an unending spiral of violence that destroys more innocent people. As my husband once said, 'The past is prophetic in that it asserts loudly that wars are poor chisels for carving out peaceful tomorrows.' Now is the time for creative, nonviolent alternatives to more brutality and destruction."[13]

On October 30, 2001, Coretta spoke to the International Conference of the Public Relations Society of America, held in Atlanta. Many of the attendees were still struggling to come to terms with the attack and to find ways to communicate about it professionally. Coretta provided the following suggestion to respond to their needs: "I know that many of us are struggling with the understandable feelings of hurt and anger toward the perpetrators of the brutality of September 11, but we, as Americans, have a special obligation not only to lift up, but also not to let this anger degenerate into hatred for any religious or ethnic group. So I think another challenge facing America's PR professionals is to help channel this anger we feel away from destructive and divisive directions into something positive and constructive."[14]

In the aftermath of this attack, the United States went to war in Afghanistan, searching for Osama Bin Laden, the organizer and instigator. Soon, President George W. Bush began to suggest the need to go to a second war in the Persian Gulf in order to unseat Sadaam Hussein, the leader of Iraq. Bush suggested that the Iraqis were in the midst of developing weapons of mass destruction and were assisting terrorist networks.

At the King Commemorative service in 2003, Coretta noted, "One day we must come to see that peace is not merely a distant goal that we seek, but a means by which we arrive at that goal. We must pursue peaceful ends through peaceful means. Martin said true peace is not merely the absence of tension, it is the presence of justice."[15] As the war went on, as long as she was able to do so, Coretta continued to speak out for peace.

NOTES

1. George M. Houser, "Freedom's Struggles Crosses Oceans and Mountains: Martin Luther King, Jr. and the Liberation Struggles in Africa and America," in *We Shall Overcome: Martin Luther King, Jr. and the Black Freedom Struggle*, ed. Peter J. Albert and Ronald Hoffman (New York: Pantheon, 1990), 182.

2. John Balzar, "U.S. Civil Rights Leaders March Against Apartheid," *Los Angeles Times*, August 13, 1995, http:///www.proquest.com (accessed August 17, 2008).

3. Kevin Sack, "Mrs. King Knew South Africa Trip a Gamble," *Atlanta Constitution*, September 20, 1986, 16-A.

4. Ibid.

5. Ibid.

6. Cynthia Durcanin, "Corporate Donors' Politics Often Contradict King Center's," *Atlanta Constitution*, January 17, 1990, A-6.

7. Harold Kennedy, "Mrs. King's Help Asked by Biafran," *Atlanta Constitution*, January 15, 1970, 12-A.

8. Coretta Scott King, Telegram to President Carter, April 6, 1978, Name File, Jimmy Carter Library, Atlanta, 1.

9. Coretta Scott King, "After the Cold War, the People," *Social Policy* 20:4 (Spring 1990), 20.

10. Mark Silk, "Coretta King Urges Israelis to Free Palestinian Activist," *Atlanta Constitution*, May 11, 1988, A-5.

11. "Gulf Notebook: General: U.S. Builds Edge," *Atlanta Journal and Constitution*, December 11, 1990, A-10.

12. Cynthia Durcanin, "Gulf War Threat, Arizona Vote Cast Shadows as King Week Starts," *Atlanta Journal and Constitution*, January 13, 1991, D-1, D-6.

13. Staff Writers, "What They Are Saying—Patriotism," *Atlanta Journal-Constitution*, September 13, 2001, A-3.

14. John Elsasser, "In Remembrance: Coretta Scott King," *Public Relations Tactics*, 13:3 (March 2006), 3.

15. Ernie Suggs, "Peace Invoked in King's Name—Speeches, Atlanta March Mark Holiday, Reflect Anti-War Movement," *Atlanta Journal-Constitution*, January 21, 2003, A-8.

Chapter 11

GUARDIANS OF MARTIN'S IMAGE AND WORDS

After Martin's assassination, Coretta worked with attorneys to handle his estate, but he did not leave a valid will. Under Georgia law, as his widow, she received the home, his personal property, and the bank accounts. One of the few assets that she inherited was Martin's papers, writings, and speeches, some of which were copyrighted. Over the years, Coretta used those materials to develop the archives, programs, and educational outreach efforts of the King Center.

MARTIN'S IMAGE

When requests came in from outside groups to use Martin's image and words, Coretta realized that she had a potential source of revenue for the Center and income for the family. In addition, once the gravesite shrine and King Center museum were established, Coretta set up a gift store to market products that included Martin's image and also to sell copies of books by him and the documentary that they had commissioned *From Memphis to Montgomery*. The gift store provided another potential source of revenue for the Center.

By the mid-1970s, the King Estate had begun to function as a separate entity from the King Center, although it always featured overlap in terms of leadership and function. Isaac Farris, Coretta's brother-in-law, oversaw operations of the King Center gift store and reviewed licensing requests. He had a background in retail, although he also maintained a full-time job as vice president of a construction company. His wife, Christine Farris, was the treasurer of the King Center.

In 1981, the King Estate filed a lawsuit against American Heritage Products, a firm that had been advertising unauthorized plastic busts of Martin for sale. American Heritage Products placed ads in *Ebony* magazine and newspapers and purported that sales of the busts would benefit the King Center. In fact, American Heritage Products was prepared to donate 3 percent of the costs of the busts, $29.95, which would generate $.90 per bust sold, but no agreement had been executed to govern the donations, and no funds had been donated yet. The Georgia Supreme Court ruled in favor of the estate, citing a 1966 case in which a dancer had recovered damages for the unauthorized use of her photograph. Intellectual property lawyers noted that this ruling was one of the strongest in the nation in terms of the right of heirs to protect the image of a person who had worked in the public arena, as it did not include a time limitation for the protection.

THE KING PAPERS

In 1981, John Silber, the president of Boston University, contacted Coretta. The Library at Boston University was in possession of 83,000 letters, documents, notes, and manuscripts that dated from Martin's graduate school days until 1964. Silber suggested that the remainder of Martin's papers be consolidated at Boston University so that they could receive proper archival care. He suggested that Martin's personal possessions as well as copies of the papers could remain at the King Center. Also in 1981, the library and archives at the King Center were opened, with a collection of approximately 100,000 King papers, as well as the papers of the SCLC, SNCC, and other civil rights organizations and individuals.

Between 1981 and 1984, Coretta and Silber corresponded toward setting up a meeting at the King Center. Coretta suggested to him that she wanted to talk about how the two entities could work together, but they never found a date to get together.

Finally, in 1985, Coretta traveled to Boston and met with Silber. Silber renewed his request that the papers be consolidated. Coretta did not agree, noting that Martin had placed his papers in Boston in 1964 out of concern that they would be destroyed during the violent resistance to civil rights activities that was ongoing in the South during the 1960s. She also added that Martin and the SCLC had organized to plan for the return of the papers to the South as early as 1967. She suggested that it was Martin's ultimate wish and assumption that his papers would end up in the South, and she added that the King Center was the place where they should be consolidated because its mission was to memorialize Martin and to carry on his work.

Over the next two years, both Coretta and Silber maintained their positions and would not back down. In 1987, Coretta filed suit. She noted that as administrator of the King Estate, her duties included "keeping these papers in proper order and seeing that they are protected for the future."[1] Boston University filed a counter-claim, requesting that Coretta surrender the King Center documents. They cited a letter of gift that Martin had signed in 1964, which stated, "In the event of my death, all such materials deposited with the University shall become from that date the absolute property of Boston University." The letter also indicated that "after the end of each calendar year, similar files of materials for an additional year should be sent to Boston University."[2]

In September 1988, Superior Court Judge John L. Murphy determined that the case would need to go to trial. He noted that the letter of gift that Martin had signed did not constitute a will and that Coretta had the right to dispute the ownership of the papers as Martin's heir. He added that the 23-year delay in Coretta's request did not invalidate her request, but that it would also be an issue during the trial.

The trial took place in April 1993. Coretta's testimony and cross-examination lasted three days. All of the King children attended and sat in the front row of the courtroom. Coretta repeated the story of the 1967 meeting to plan for the return of the papers. She asserted that the group (which was made up of Benjamin Mays, Daddy King, Harold Wachtel, and Stanley Levison) told Martin that he should inform Boston University of his desire to see the papers come back to the South. But Martin had not fulfilled this request out of concern for the feelings of his mentor, Harold DeWolf, who had cultivated the donation of the papers. Coretta was the only attendee from the meeting available to testify to what happened and Martin's wishes.

The Boston University attorneys also questioned Coretta about the condition of the papers at the King Center. Coretta noted that the Center only retained an archival consultant on staff. She also admitted that she had stored many of Martin's papers for nearly a decade in the basement of her Atlanta home, which did not have a dehumidifier or fire suppression system.

Coretta's attorneys introduced as evidence a letter from scholar David Garrow, who expressed concern with the care that the King papers were receiving in Boston. He had worked with those papers during research for his Pulitzer Prize–winning book *Bearing the Cross*. To rebut, Taylor Branch, who had used the same archives while researching his book *Parting the Waters*, testified as the first witness for Boston University.

Ultimately, the jury voted 10 to 2 in Boston University's favor. Coretta appealed to the state Supreme Court, citing that "moral justice" had failed.

Martin Luther King III echoed his mother's sentiments and pointed out that it seemed inappropriate to have to go to court over items that should belong to them as the heirs of Martin. However, in 1995, that court upheld the ruling of the lower court. The papers that Martin donated to Boston University would remain there; the papers in the King Center Collection would remain there; and the King Family would retain copyright to all of the papers (a fact that had never been in question).

Also in 1985, Coretta established a project to edit and publish Martin's papers. She identified Clayborne Carson of Stanford University as the editor and project leader, and he began compiling and editing Martin's writings for publication. The King Center received several federal grants to support their work. Coretta wanted the project to be based out of the King Center, but Carson set up the main office at Stanford University, where he was a tenured professor. He hired a staff of graduate and undergraduate students to work on the project, which grew to fill a wing of Cypress Hall on the Stanford campus. He did, however, also organize a project office at the King Center and relationships with archivists and librarians at Emory University.

MARTIN'S PLAGIARISM

As the staff of the papers project meticulously annotated for publication Martin's work from graduate school at Boston University, including his dissertation, they found occasions in which he incorporated material from others' writings without citation. By 1988, project archivists recognized this plagiarism. Clayborne Carson intended for the news to become public through an article in the *Journal of American History*, an academic publication, however, it broke in *The Wall Street Journal* and the *Los Angeles Times* on November 9, 1990.

Coretta did not comment publicly on the findings. King Center staffers noted that they remained committed to the work of the project, so that there could be a full scholarly analysis of Martin's contributions. She did provide the King Papers Project note cards from the era of his dissertation, which indicated his style of collecting references. Editors wondered if Coretta could shed additional light on his writing process because she typed his dissertation, but she continued to withhold comment.

Some civil rights veterans disputed the accuracy of the charges, suggesting that Martin's writings included examples of the blending of voices, a practice common to African American preaching. Former special assistant Bernard Lee lashed out at the scholars, noting they were "zealous students" and "academically constipated."[3] On the other hand, Dr. Joseph Lowery, who was serving as president of the SCLC, noted, "It's inevitable with every hero that, as time goes by, people put in proper perspective their humanness, and that's what is happening to Dr. King."[4] The family of Dr. Jack Boozer, whose dissertation from Boston University was one of the uncited sources for Martin's writings, noted that "he was honored that he could have been of some help to Martin Luther King."[5] Clayborne Carson added that these findings pertained to Martin's academic work during graduate school in theology when he was wrestling with defining a conception of God that worked for him. It did not deal with his activism or civil rights leadership. Ultimately the papers project went forward, and scholars continued to organize and publish Martin's writings. Clayborne Carson noted that the volumes would serve as "another monument . . . to King, and a very positive monument for the most part."[6]

LAWSUITS OVER MARTIN'S IMAGE

It is within the context of the lawsuit over control of Martin's papers, as well as the accusations of his plagiarism, that lawyers representing the King Estate began to be more aggressive in controlling the unauthorized use of Martin's words. In 1992, they wrote Henry Hampton of Blackside, Inc., the producers of *Eyes on the Prize*, claiming that the documentary series used Martin's image without proper permission. Coretta had been interviewed and footage of her interview had also been used in the documentary, but what the King Estate was concerned about was the historical footage of Martin's speeches and sermons. Hampton offered the King Estate $100,000 in hope of settling, but the Estate did not accept the offer and requested a much higher licensing fee. In response Hampton filed a lawsuit in Boston against the King Estate, noting that their threats impeded Blackside's freedom of speech in developing a second series of episodes. Another argument that Hampton used was that public broadcasting stations were afraid to air *Eyes on the Prize* during Black History Month in 1993 due to the King Family's threats. Dexter King argued that Hampton's lawsuit was an attack on his family. He also noted that *Eyes on the Prize* had usurped the earning potential of their authorized documentary, *From Montgomery to Memphis*, and that *Eyes on the Prize* was being sold at commercial outlets such as Blockbuster. The King Estate and Hampton eventually settled their case, but Hampton was still upset because he had seen his documentary series as a tribute to Martin's work and the civil rights movement.

In 1992, the King Estate also sued in Los Angeles Superior Court to prevent the auctioning of an outline of a speech that Martin had left on a reporter's writing tablet. In 1993, they sued *USA Today* for reprinting portions of the "I Have a Dream" speech on the thirtieth anniversary of the

March on Washington. *USA Today* settled the case out of court, paying the Estate a licensing fee and legal costs.

Less than a week after he testified in the trial over the Boston University King Papers, Taylor Branch received a letter reminding him that commercial uses of Dr. King's copyrighted words required a written licensing agreement with his heirs. While the King Center continued to allow educational and nonprofit organizations to reproduce Martin's words without charge, scholars and writers in the media began to question the timing and motivation of their efforts to control and license Martin's image.

In 1994, Dexter King replaced Coretta as president and CEO of the King Center. For the second time, at age 67, Coretta was attempting to retire. This was also the period in which the family was engaged in controversy with the National Park Service (NPS) about the visitors' center. In a speech Dexter noted:

> The King Center is the spiritual and institutional guardian of the King legacy. Our main goal is to educate the public about, and to perpetuate and promote, my father's message of non-violence to people around the world. To achieve this goal, we must protect my father's intellectual property—the images, writings, and speeches that embody his message. . . . Land is the real estate of the past. Intellectual property is the real estate of now. If you stand back and let others steal his material, then you're affecting every minority writer, every songwriter, every composer, every artist, every storyteller, every creative person—all of that—gone.[7]

Dexter arranged for Intellectual Properties Management (IPM), a firm created by his friend and advisor Phillip Jones, to manage the King Estate, handle licensing agreements, and plan for the marketing of Martin's images and works. IPM was incorporated on November 4, 1994. In early 1995, the King Estate discontinued their relationship with the law firm that had handled licensing and marketing for 20 years, noting that their fees had become too expensive. Yet, in February 1995, the *Atlanta Constitution* reported that payroll at the King Center had more than tripled in two years and that this increase had been a factor in the Center running a $2 million deficit.[8]

On January 24, 1995, Coretta sent a letter to Lloyd Davis asking that the Federal King Holiday Commission cease initiatives. She noted the change in leadership at the King Center and suggested that fundraising or activities of the Commission would be in direct competition with the

King Center. "Any opportunities regarding the name, image, and/or likeness of Martin's would jeopardize our fundraising abilities, as well as our mission and purpose, if a control was not put into place. Until this can be re-accessed along with the vision, any plans should be forestalled."[9] She reasserted that the King Center should be the preserver and presenter of Martin's image and that even the King Commission should have to license use of the images for educational materials through the King Center. It is ironic that in fall 1994, Congress had renewed the charter of the Federal Holiday Commission until 1999, with an increase in their appropriation of $50,000.

The minutes of the Operations Committee of the King Commission present a contentious discussion between the members of the Commission, who thought they were acting in good faith, and Coretta and Dexter. Dexter was the main spokesman for the family. He suggested that Coretta had been in poor health and that another motivation for the change was the effort to relieve pressure on her. The final outcome, after a couple more difficult meetings, was the disbanding of the King Commission in December 1996.

The Commission had served as a liaison for 35 state and local commissions around the country, coordinating holiday themes and celebration activities. The disbanding of the commission left those duties for the King Center, but during days of its own financial struggles, it was difficult for them to fulfill that role.

In 1996, the estate sued CBS for marketing a videotape that contained excerpts of the "I Have a Dream Speech." The King Estate's case was complicated due to the fact that the news footage in question had been recorded in 1963 by CBS reporters. CBS claimed rights as a news organization to use its own material, even if the speech in question had been copyrighted. The King Estate countered that the news footage was being repackaged into a commercial product, a documentary series, making the use not covered under the fair use doctrine of copyright law. This case settled in 2000, with an undisclosed amount of money being paid to the King Estate and with CBS retaining the right to use its news footage in the video documentary. In his autobiography, Dexter King noted that the family spent approximately a million dollars in legal fees in conjunction with this case.

TIME WARNER PUBLISHING AGREEMENT

In 1997, the King Estate announced that it was entering into an exclusive publishing agreement with Warner Books, a division of Time Warner. The official announcement press conference was in New York, with Coretta, Dexter, and Gerald Levin, Chairman of Time Warner in attendance. The arrangement would provide for the publication of a biography of Martin to be developed by Clayborne Carson using words from the Martin Luther King, Jr. Papers Project, a second autobiography by Coretta, and a memoir by Dexter. In addition, there would be an Internet site and compact discs and CD-ROM of Martin's writings and speeches. The exact figures of the agreement were not disclosed, but estimates suggested it would generate up to $10 million per year by 2000. At the press conference, Coretta announced, "This is a great day for the legacy of Martin Luther King, Jr. I believe that this historic agreement will make an extraordinary contribution to promoting my husband's teachings in nonviolence."[10] Gerald Levin concurred, "This [King's writings] is a relatively unexposed treasure. I believe that the civil rights movement of the 1960s will emerge as a pivotal period in American history."[11]

Coretta, Dexter, and Gerald Levin all noted that the deal would generate funds that would help modernize the King Center. Dexter suggested that raising his father's stature, through new published works, would heighten awareness of the Center. However, all were clear that the funding would not flow directly to the Center but would rather pass through the Estate.

In 1998, Dexter announced the establishment of a second nonprofit the National Institute for Community Empowerment (also known as the Community Empowerment Institute or CEI). It would assume responsibility for providing training in nonviolence to community groups, which had been handled by the King Center. In a press conference, he stated that "CEI was born out of the Kingian philosophy of creating the beloved community." He also compared CEI to the Historic District Development Corporation, a preservation and redevelopment organization that had grown out of Coretta's work in setting up the King Center.[12] Coretta did not speak at this announcement, although it occurred as part of the King Holiday festivities, which she attended. According to records of the Georgia Secretary of State's office, the National Institute for Community Empowerment voluntarily disbanded as a nonprofit organization in August 2005.

THE FATE OF THE KING PAPERS AND THE KING CENTER

In February 1998, the King Estate began negotiations with the NPS about buying Coretta's home and possessions as well as the King Center property. In early 1999, NPS staff began to develop an inventory of the possessions in order that they could be appraised. Plans were also initiated to raise private funds to purchase the materials from the King Estate so that they could be displayed in the King site visitors' center, and thoughts were given to making the King home an additional facility of the historic district. The sales did not go forward, and the NPS continued to work in partnership with the King Estate to interpret the historic district.

In 1997, the Library of Congress contacted the King Estate about acquiring the King Center collection of Martin's papers. The Library of Congress's interest in Martin's papers dated back to 1967, when they made initial contact. The U.S. Senate passed a bill to allow for the purchase in October 1999, and the bill went to the House of Representatives for consideration. Representative James Clyburn, chairman of the Congressional Black Caucus, managed the bill and introduced legislation to provide for an appropriation to underwrite the sale. Sotheby's auction house appraised the documents at $30 million. Coretta indicated that she would be willing to sell them for $10–$20 million as a gift to the nation.

The proposed sale hit two snags. First, the King Center intended to keep their collection of papers from civil rights organizations such as the SCLC and SNCC. Archivists and historians were uncomfortable with separating them, especially with the separation of Martin's papers and the SCLC papers because Martin was the founding president of the SCLC. It seemed difficult to ascertain which papers were Martin's personal property and which were the property of SCLC.

More significantly, the King Estate insisted that it would retain copyright to Martin's papers because they would be accepting a price for them significantly below appraised value. While the Library of Congress admitted that some donors retained copyright to their materials, Congressional leaders countered that purchasing at a discount price was not the same thing as accepting a donation. They were uncomfortable with public tax dollars going to obtain possession of materials for which the Library of Congress would not be able to provide reproduction rights. Ultimately, the deal fell apart.

In 2001, the Estate negotiated with the national King Memorial Foundation regarding the use of Martin's image. The Foundation, which was founded by brothers of Martin's fraternity, Alpha Phi Alpha, had been working toward a memorial on the National Mall in Washington, D.C. since 1984. Media reports suggested that the King Estate was requesting to receive a portion of the funds raised for the memorial in exchange for the use of Martin's image. Dexter countered that the Estate's interest was in negotiating a permissions agreement that would control how the corporate donors to the Foundation would have access to Martin's image. Any funds that were derived, if licensing fees were involved, would go to support the King Center. Ultimately, the parties reached an agreement, and fundraising and planning for the memorial continued.

In 2003, the King Estate contracted with Sotheby's auction house to manage the sale of a collection of approximately 10,000 of Martin's papers, manuscripts, and books. The aim was to generate funds to support the King Center and to pay legal fees. The sale was to be by "private treaty," which meant the family could accept or reject potential buyers. In addition, the Estate would continue to remain copyright. Ultimately, a buyer that they were comfortable with did not emerge, and the sale did not go through.

After Coretta's death in January 2006, the Estate again posted the papers for sale at Sotheby's. In June 2006, a nonprofit consortium organized by Atlanta Mayor Shirley Franklin purchased the papers for $32 million. SunTrust Bank provided loans to guarantee that amount. Once the loans would be repaid, the papers would become the property of Morehouse College and be housed at the Atlanta University Center Robert Woodruff Library and Archives. A first display of the papers occurred at the Atlanta History Center in summer 2007, and it drew over 70,000 people.

In summer 2008, the Atlanta King Papers consortium refinanced the loan from SunTrust Bank because they still needed to raise $8 million to complete the repayment of the purchase price for the papers.

In addition, in July 2008 Bernice and Martin III filed a lawsuit in Superior Court in Atlanta against Dexter challenging his actions and management of funds as executor of the King Estate. Reacting to the news, Joseph Lowery noted, "It is sad that the King legacy, which espouses negotiation, reconciliation and love has to have this," Lowery said. "But they will get over it. I am hoping they remember who they are and whose they are. Let's all engage in prayer that it will be settled."[13] Juanita Abernathy added, "It tugs at the heartstrings, because I know that their parents would not want this. They taught their children to get along."[14]

In August 2008, Dexter filed a countersuit against Martin III and Bernice, on behalf of the King Center. His case charged that Martin III and Bernice had created nonprofits that were in competition with the King Center. In addition, they had used King Center facilities for programs or fundraising that were for the other efforts instead of the King Center.

It will be some time before these cases come to trial or the parties find a way to settle. The case is complicated by the status of Martin's estate because he died without a will. Though Coretta began to speak of the King Estate in the 1970s, it was not legally incorporated until 1994, with

Coretta and Dexter as the main executors. When Coretta died, she had a will, with Yolanda as executrix, but that will dated back to 1984, prior to the legal incorporation of the King Estate and negotiations of complex arrangements like the Time Warner publishing deal. In addition, Yolanda's death in 2007 added to the dispute over who would control Martin's and Coretta's estates.

As of January 2009, the legal and personal disputes continue among the siblings. At the heart of the dispute currently is control of Coretta's personal papers (which likely contain materials written by Martin). On behalf of the King Estate, Dexter contracted with an author to develop an authorized biography of Coretta, just prior to her death. After her death, the Estate proposed for the author to have access to Coretta's personal papers. Bernice and Martin III refused to turn over the papers that were in their possession, indicating that Coretta had not been comfortable working with the potential author and that they felt the papers should remain private for the time being. They also objected to Dexter's management of the King Estate corporation and his failure to convene meetings of the shareholders (which included them). Ultimately, the publishing company cancelled the contract for the authorized biography. During the hearings of the competing lawsuits, an Atlanta judge ordered that a special master be appointed to audit the personal papers in preparation for their ultimate disposition. The judge also ruled that Bernice and Martin III would have to pay some legal fees for Dexter, due to their delay in providing access to the papers. As Ben Smith wrote in the *Atlanta Journal-Constitution*, "It could take months, if not years before the personal papers of the late Coretta Scott King become public."[15]

In the midst of these disputes, the status of the King Estate and the fate of the King Center remain unresolved as the heirs attempt to work through their personal differences and find a structure that makes the most sense for the future.

NOTES

1. Gayle White, "Widow Claims King Feared Loss of Papers," *Atlanta Constitution*, December 12, 1987, 5E.

2. "Flap Over MLK Papers Heats Up Between King's Widow, College," *Atlanta Constitution*, April 9, 1988, A-7.

3. Cynthia Durcanin, "Plagiarism Revelation Splits King's Followers," *Atlanta Constitution*, November 11, 1990, A-8.

4. Frances Schwartzkopf and Cynthia Durcanin, "King's Plagiarism Rocks Scholars, Supporters," *Atlanta Constitution*, November 10, 1990, A-1.

5. Ann Hardie, "Family: Scholar Honored to Help King," *Atlanta Constitution,* November 11, 1990, A-8.

6. Ann Hardie, "Scholar Tested by Controversy Over King Papers," *Atlanta Constitution,* December 2, 1990, A-20.

7. Dexter King, *Growing Up King: An Intimate Memoir* (New York: Warner Books, 2003), 201.

8. Mark Sherman, "King Deficit Is Linked to Payroll," *Atlanta Constitution,* February 6, 1995, A-1.

9. Coretta Scott King, Memo to Lloyd Davis, January 24, 1995; minutes of Martin Luther King, Jr. Federal Holiday Commission, National Archives–SE Region, Morrow, Georgia, 1.

10. Michael Eric Dyson, *I May Not Get There With You* (New York: The Free Press, 2000), 275.

11. Charles Haddad, "An 'unexposed treasure,'" *Atlanta Constitution,* January 9, 1997, E-1.

12. S. A. Reid, "Making Dream Reality," *Atlanta Constitution,* January 18, 1998, C4.

13. Ernie Suggs, "MLK's Heirs in Legal Dispute; Dexter King Sued by Two Siblings over How He Handled Funds," *Atlanta Journal-Constitution,* July 12, 2008, A1, A8.

14. Ernie Suggs and Bob Keefe, "Siblings Suit Hits Dexter King Hard," *Atlanta Journal-Constitution,* July 13, 2008, F1, F3.

15. Ben Smith, "King Siblings' Battle Could Linger: Their Mother's Personal Papers: Dexter King, Bernice King, MLK III Still at Odds over Use, Despite Judge's Ruling," *Atlanta Journal-Constitution,* January 2, 2009, C1.

Chapter 12

REOPENING THE KING ASSASSINATION

Martin was killed on April 4, 1968, while standing on a balcony of the Lorraine Hotel in Memphis. A bullet struck him in the throat, fired by a powerful rifle. The FBI and the Memphis police initiated an investigation. In a nearby building, they found evidence, with fingerprints, including a map of Atlanta, clothing, a rifle, and scope. The room had been rented to a person claiming to be Eric S. Gault, but the fingerprints were identified as belonging to James Earl Ray, a fugitive from a Missouri penitentiary.

THE TRIAL OF JAMES EARL RAY

Ray was arrested at Heathrow Airport in London on June 10, 1968. The U.S. government brought him back to Memphis to face charges, including the federal crime of violating Martin's civil rights and the state crime of first degree murder. Before the case came to trial, Ray pled guilty to the murder charge. He hoped that this plea would prevent him from receiving the death penalty. Coretta and Ralph Abernathy also spoke out against the death penalty for Ray, noting that Martin was opposed to the death penalty and believed in forgiveness.

Tennessee legal practice required that the charges and penalty be entered into the record in front of a jury. On March 10, 1969, a state court in Memphis selected a jury that included two African Americans. Judge W. Preston Battle talked to the jury before they were seated and told them about Ray's plea and his proposed sentence of 99 years in prison. After listening to testimony of Samuel Kyles and Chauncey Eskridge (friends of Martin's who had been at the scene of the crime), as well as the Shelby

County Medical Examiner, a Memphis city police detective, and an FBI agent, the jury agreed to accept Ray's guilty plea and the judge's sentence.

Prosecutors suggested that Ray acted out of racism and that he had stalked Martin for a period prior to the assassination. They also noted that evidence suggested that Ray acted alone. However, in a statement after the close of the case, Judge Battle noted,

> Of course this is not conclusive evidence that there was no conspiracy. It merely means that there is not sufficient evidence available to make a case of probable cause. However, if this defendant was a member of a conspiracy to kill the decedent, no member of such conspiracy can ever live in peace or security or lie down to pleasant dreams, because in this state there is no statute of limitations in capital cases such as this.[1]

DOUBTS ARISE

Coretta and Daddy King did not attend Ray's trial. However, in response to the verdict, Coretta suggested that they held doubts as to whether Ray's conviction would bring a complete end to the story. She noted that "for the family, there is a sense of emotional relief" as they had been "spared a trial, which would compel us to relive the fearfully tragic events of his death. But we realize that it is but a respite." She also added that Ray's guilty pleas "cannot be allowed to close the case, to end the search for the many fingers which helped pull the trigger." She called on the people of Tennessee and the U.S. government "to continue until all who are responsible for this crime have been apprehended. Not until then can the conscience of this nation rest."[2]

Ralph Abernathy added that Ray's guilty plea added to his belief that there was a conspiracy behind the assassination. He suggested that the conspiracy tied into broad social causes, rather than particular individuals or organizations. "The SCLC is committed to remain alert and vigilant until justice is meted out to all of the perpetrators. We believe that racism, which infects our whole society, was in truth the principal assassin."[3] This echoed a statement that Abernathy had made at the first commemorative service for Martin in January 1969, when he implied that society was "sick" and that it was the symptoms of racism, poverty, and violence that led to Martin's death more so than an individual killer.

After Ray went to jail, the visibility of the assassination case died down and fell out of the public spotlight. Still, King family members and close associates of Martin's wondered how James Earl Ray could have accomplished the task by himself. In his memoir, Dexter King recalled that Martin's brother, A. D., often said, "There's more to this than meets the eye, and one day God will judge it all."[4] Coretta did not speak out frequently on the topic, rather focusing her attention on raising the children and establishing the King Center.

JAMES EARL RAY'S RESPONSE

In addition, Ray recanted his guilty plea within three days of conviction, and he began writing to Judge Battle. Battle died on March 31, 1969, which ended his possible involvement. James continued to seek a new trial, filing appeals with state and federal courts that lasted until 1976.

One of Ray's claims was that he had not been given adequate legal advice and representation. His first lawyer, Arthur Hanes, served as a party to a three-way agreement between Ray and author William Bradford Huie, which granted Huie the literary rights for Ray's story that became the 1970 book *He Slew the Dreamer*. Hanes' portion and Ray's portion later went to Ray's second lawyer, Percy Foreman. When questioned about the conflict of interest that this contract represented, Foreman suggested that the Hanes/Foreman portion was to cover Ray's legal expenses, whereas the Ray portion was being held in trust so that it would be sheltered in the event that Coretta sued Ray in civil court for damages related to Martin's death. Of course, Coretta never pursued such an option.

In 1977, the House of Representatives set up a Select Committee on Assassinations, which investigated Martin's assassination as well as that of John F. Kennedy. This committee was one of several Congressional oversight committees set up in the aftermath of the Watergate scandal, seeking to prevent governmental agencies from using power to interfere with the rights of individual citizens and political organizations. In addition, the focus on assassinations grew out of the proliferation of conspiracy theories that had begun to emerge in relation to the Kennedy and King assassinations.

WILLIAM PEPPER GETS INVOLVED

In June 1977, Ray attempted to escape from prison, but he was shortly recaptured. In 1978, attorney and journalist William F. Pepper met with James Earl Ray in prison, accompanied by Ralph Abernathy and an expert in interpreting body language. Pepper was a veteran of the civil rights movement, whose path had crossed with Martin's in 1966.

In addition, Pepper served as the executive director of the National Conference for New Politics (NCNP), a coalition advocating the end to the Vietnam War. Martin had begun to speak out against the Vietnam War publicly in 1967. He was also in the midst of planning the Poor People's Campaign. Pepper remembered that he had discussions with Martin about Martin joining Dr. Benjamin Spock and forming a ticket to run for President in order to highlight an antiwar and antipoverty platform. The NCNP coalition splintered at their convention over Labor Day weekend 1967, due to the presence of an outspoken Black Power contingent. Via the SCLC, Martin continued his work toward the Poor People's Campaign and sought to build another multiracial coalition, but his assassination prevented his seeing that campaign to fruition.

It was because of this involvement in New Left politics, and his knowledge of the FBI's use of surveillance and counter-intelligence operations, that William Pepper built a suspicion that a conspiracy was behind the death of Martin. During his meeting with James Earl Ray and Ralph Abernathy, Ray told them that he was not the assassin and that he had been set up through the involvement of a man he knew only as "Raul." After the meeting, Pepper and Abernathy agreed that Ray had been set up, and Pepper began an investigation that led him to confirm his suspicions of conspiracy.

In March 1979, the House Select Committee on Assassinations issued their final report on Martin's case. After examining the evidence and hearing testimony, they reaffirmed that James Earl Ray had acted as a lone gunman. If there were conspirators with Ray in the crime, the evidence did not support their identification.

Still, William Pepper continued to conduct his own investigations of the case. Though he moved to England in 1981 and began practicing international law, he kept an interest in the Ray case and followed Ray's efforts to obtain a new trial. In 1988, he became Ray's lawyer, filing another appeal and seeking to introduce new evidence. The request was denied. He took the appeal to the U.S. Supreme Court in 1989, but it was also denied.

In 1992, Pepper contracted with a British production group to conduct a televised trial of James Earl Ray. It aired on April 4, 1993. Pepper served as the defense and a former federal court judge was the prosecutor. A group of Americans composed the jury, and they listened to evidence from a "prosecutor" and a "defense attorney." Ray, of course, was not there, and the King family was not involved. However, the jury declared Ray "not guilty."

THE KING FAMILY GETS INVOLVED

In 1995, Pepper published a book, *Orders to Kill*. It made a case for the involvement of a military "special forces" group in Martin's assassination.

He mailed copies of the book with cover letters to Coretta and her children and to Christine and Isaac Farris.

In 1996, James Earl Ray was diagnosed with cirrhosis, the result of long-undiagnosed and untreated Hepatitis C. Pepper and Ray's brothers began legal efforts for him to receive a transplant, which is the only thing that would have saved him, but such heroic medical efforts were not permitted for a prisoner with a life sentence. The Ray family informed the *New York Times* of the situation, and they approached the King family for a comment, as journalists had traditionally done when there was news about Ray.

This time the family broke its practice of saying "no comment." Isaac Farris, Jr., Christine's son, was the first member of the family to read *Orders to Kill*, and he had been impressed, so he suggested that his cousins also take a look. In January 1997, Yolanda and Isaac reached out to Pepper. Dexter, Isaac, and Dexter's advisor, Phillip Jones, met with Pepper in early February 1997, and on February 13, the family held a press conference where they announced that they would support Ray receiving a new trial so that new evidence could be brought forward and entered into the record. Dexter also traveled to Memphis and met with Ray.

Coretta testified in support of a motion that Pepper filed to test the weapon presumed to have been used to shoot Martin, "We call for the trial that never happened . . . If we fail to seize this fading opportunity for justice to be served, the tragedy will be compounded by the failure of the legal system."[5] She also added, "Most importantly, for the sake of healing and reconciliation, I appeal to you on behalf of the King family as well as millions of Americans concerned about truth and justice in this case, to expeditiously set and conduct a trial for Mr. James Earl Ray."[6]

Also in 1997, the ABC News' program *Turning Point* explored the Ray case and Pepper's argument. They undercut Pepper's claims via interviews with military officials. Other media articles also portrayed the family's decision in a negative light and noted it was not in line with their usual standards of dignity to be connected with such conspiracy theories.

James Earl Ray died on April 23, 1998, without ever having another trial. Pepper and the King family continued to search for other channels to learn more about the assassination. They asked for President Bill Clinton's help, citing the model of the South African Truth and Reconciliation Commission. Such a group would be outside of government but would have subpoena powers and the ability to grant immunity in return for testimony. Growing out of their experiences with the FBI, they suspected governmental involvement in the assassination. However, President Clinton referred the request to the Department of Justice.

THE CONSPIRACY TRIAL AND LOYD JOWERS

Meanwhile, the Kings and Pepper determined another route to reopening the assassination case before a jury. They sued Loyd Jowers, the owner of a restaurant across from the Lorraine Motel, and other unknown conspirators in civil court. They sought $100 in damages. Coretta noted that this option made sense, as they had "come too far not to complete this effort."[7]

William Pepper had interviewed Loyd Jowers several times about his knowledge of the case over the years. Jowers had asserted that meetings to coordinate the assassination took place in his restaurant, Jim's Grill. Pepper had arranged for Dexter and Andrew Young to meet with Jowers, who was elderly and in poor health. From interview to interview, his story would shift slightly, and this presented another obstacle to Pepper making a clear case.

The trial started on November 16, 1999. Coretta was the first witness. Pepper asked her to describe Martin's plans to return to Memphis to lead a nonviolent march with the sanitation workers, since the first march had ended in violence. He also asked her to reflect on Martin's plans for the Poor People's Campaign and his opposition to the Vietnam War. He asked her how these commitments of Martin's had affected his depiction in the media as well as his abilities to raise funds for the SCLC. Pepper later drew a parallel between the stands that Martin took and the impact that they made on him and the stands that Coretta and the children were taking and the impact that these stands were having on the King Center.

A key question of Pepper's was why were the family members bringing this issue to trial 31 years later? Coretta responded:

> Well, it has only been recently that we realized the extent of Mr. Jowers' involvement. So we felt that it was important to bring it now. We're all getting older, I'll say, and, of course, we wanted to be able to get the truth, as much of it as we can, out before it gets later. I don't know how much longer any of us will be around. That's not given. But the fact is that my family, my children and I—I've always felt that somehow the truth would be known, and I hoped that I would live to see it. And it is important I think for the sake of healing for so many people, my family, for other people, for the nation. I think Martin Luther King, Jr., served this nation. He was a servant. He gave his—he willingly gave his life if it was necessary. It is important to know, actually not because we feel a sense of revenge—we

never have. We have no feeling of bitterness or hatred toward anybody. But just the fact that if we know the truth, we can be free, and we can go on with our lives.[8]

Coretta did not attend the rest of the trial. Members of the family rotated in and out. Dexter was the last witness for the prosecution, and his testimony reiterated the full case that included conspiracy within Memphis circles, conspiracy involving military and federal government circles, and a cover-up. The defense admitted that Jowers had some awareness of a conspiracy, but that he had not known the aim was to assassinate Martin. His restaurant, a public venue, was the scene of meetings and planning, but this was not out of his own arrangement.

The trial lasted four weeks long. A total of 70 people testified, either in person, via videotape, or deposition. The judge dismissed the jury to deliberate, identifying three questions for their consideration:

1. Did the defendant Loyd Jowers participate in a conspiracy to do harm to Dr. Martin Luther King, Jr.? If yes:
2. Did you also find that others including governmental agencies were parties to this conspiracy as alleged by the defendant?
3. What is the total amount of damages to be awarded to the plaintiffs?

After about an hour of deliberation, the jury returned with the answers of "yes" to questions one and two and damages totaling $100. The judge assigned the responsibility of paying the judgment to Loyd Jowers at 30 percent and other (unknown) conspirators at 70 percent.

In response to the verdict, Coretta and the family held a press conference at the King Center. Coretta noted that she was relieved that the trial had come to a speedy conclusion and that she could now move on, having had some of her questions answered. She quoted Martin, "The moral arch of the universe is long, but it bends towards justice." Dexter served as the main family spokesman, "while my heart is heavy, this is sweet, because we finally know what happened. Sweet because the family has been vindicated. Sweet because we can say 'free at last.' "[9]

With William Pepper, the family indicated plans to advocate for changes in textbook accounts of the King assassination to include references to conspiracy. However, six months later, the U.S. Department of Justice announced that after an investigation, they found no evidence of a conspiracy. Specifically, they discounted the notion that Loyd Jowers had been paid by a mobster to hire a sharpshooter other than James Earl Ray to assassinate Martin. They also discounted claims by former FBI agent Donald Wilson who had come forward and indicated he found items in James Earl Ray's car in Atlanta that validated the existence of the shadowy "Raul" figure.

The family was disappointed but not surprised. Martin III and Andrew Young served as the spokespeople for the family, noting that it is difficult for the government to investigate itself. Undoubtedly, the family's awareness of the FBI's surveillance of Martin and COINTELPRO against the civil rights movement contributed to their willingness to believe in the existence of a conspiracy, even a conspiracy that involved governmental forces. Also, the children had come of age in a post-Watergate world, when journalists had exposed governmental involvement in many underhanded actions, including political assassinations.

NOTES

1. Celestine Sibley, "Ray Gets 99-Year Term After King Guilty Plea: No Plot Found in Slaying: 33 Year Wait for a Parole," *Atlanta Constitution*, March 11, 1969, 9.

2. "Widow Says It's Not Over: Case Pressed by Mrs. King," *Atlanta Constitution*, March 11, 1969, 1.

3. Ibid.

4. Dexter King, *Growing Up King: An Intimate Memoir* (New York: Warner Books, 2003), 74.

5. William Pepper, *An Act of State* (London: Verso, 2003), 86.

6. Ibid., 89.

7. Ibid., 98.

8. Transcript, Martin Luther King, Jr. Conspiracy Trial, Volume 2, November 16, 1995, http://www.thekingcenter.org/news/trial/Volume2.html.

9. Ernie Suggs, "After Three Decades Family Can Finally Say, 'Free at Last,'" *Atlanta Constitution*, December 10, 1999, E-1.

Chapter 13

CORETTA'S LAST ACTS

Coretta celebrated her 66th birthday on April 27, 1993. The following week, 1,500 people attended "A Tribute to Coretta Scott King," which was a $150 per plate fundraiser for the King Center. Atlanta businessman Herman J. Russell chaired the program, and he noted that this was the first fundraiser specifically devoted to Coretta's work and to showing "appreciation for the woman who has devoted the past 25 years of her life to the elimination of the triple evils: poverty, racism, and war."[1]

Singer Dionne Warwick and television talk show host Phil Donahue cohosted the four-hour salute, which featured music by Stevie Wonder, Take 6, and Sweet Honey and the Rock; videotaped messages from Cicely Tyson and President and Mrs. Jimmy Carter; and speeches by Andrew Young, Joseph Lowery, and Betty Shabazz. In addition, archival footage from the King Center was shown, including a clip of Martin reflecting on their first date and how he recognized her quickly as a worthy partner in his work.

Coretta sat at a table between Bernice and her sister, Edythe. She smiled and laughed at stories that those paying tribute told, but she was also touched and brought to tears by some of the statements. One such one was from Sidney Poitier, "Through you, our ancestors pull at our hearts, and we remember."[2]

The evening was a long-overdue recognition of Coretta for her work in preserving Martin's memory and promoting his legacy. It was also a beginning for attention being paid to Coretta for her own life and work.

Ironically, it came during the same period that she was embattled with Boston University regarding the ownership of Martin's papers. The same week as the tribute, Coretta testified. The cross-examination was difficult because she admitted that she kept a portion of Martin's papers under less-than-optimal preservation conditions in the basement of her home. She also was forced to admit that there was no written evidence to support her contention that Martin desired to take back the donation of papers that he made to Boston University in 1964.

CORETTA'S BURDENS

In addition, the early 1990s saw pressures increase on Coretta to raise funds to maintain the King Center's facilities and enhance it as a vehicle for interpreting Martin's life and work. The site had become a popular destination for tourists, although it lacked infrastructure such as bathrooms and parking. Coretta continued to pursue opportunities to raise funds through public and private sources. Yet, she did not ever identify ongoing sources of support that would provide for maintenance of the facilities and endowment of programs.

Dexter replaced Coretta as chairman and CEO of the King Center for the second time in January 1995. He had been elected to the post the previous fall, and his role as spokesman for the family had increased during the debate and negotiations with the National Park Service over plans for a visitors center prior to the Olympics.

In a speech on King Day when he was inaugurated, Dexter stated, "My father delivered to his generation political freedom. I would like to deliver to my generation economic freedom."[3] He recognized the King Estate and Martin's intellectual property as important tools in building that legacy. He also saw the intellectual property as an asset that should be exploited through licensing and repackaging so that he could raise funds for the King Center in new ways. He ramped up the licensing work of the King Estate and incorporated IPM as a vehicle for handling these transactions.

The effort to police and more tightly control Martin's intellectual property was one of the issues in the debate with the National Park Service. Ironically, one casualty of this disagreement was a proposed exhibit to focus on Coretta's life and work.

Dexter was also central to the debate about the fate of the Federal King Holiday Commission, which came to a head in March 1995. During a meeting of the Commission's Operating Committee, Dexter implied that his mother had been ill and needed to retire from the position of commission chair as she had also retired from leadership of the King Center. Coretta's illnesses had not been reported in the media, but at the age of 68 it could be expected that she would have some health concerns.

In July 1996, Coretta agreed to an interview with Hollis Towns of the *Atlanta Constitution*, which updated the public on her postretirement efforts. Coretta noted that she still spent several hours a week at the King Center, though she also had begun to devote more time to visiting with family and to pursuing her own goals. She was at work on a memoir about her life after Martin, and she also wanted to return to singing, with plans to record an album. At the time of Coretta's death, the second memoir remained incomplete.

CORETTA'S LIFESTYLE

Coretta also shared to Hollis Towns that she had become a vegetarian, following the influence of Dexter, and she found that her diet and exercise helped her feel better. Her daily schedule, which began at 7 a.m., included time for meditation, prayer, talking on the telephone with friends, and watching CNN. She continued to receive many requests to speak, and she accepted them as she could, in order to earn honoraria. She drew no pension from the King Center because she had not accepted a salary during her tenure there.

She suffered from poor circulation in her legs and wore special stockings to prevent clots. She had an assistant to help around the house, but when her daughter Bernice was ill with pneumonia, she spent time at Bernice's home, cooking, washing clothes, and nursing "her baby" back to health. She also continued to buy clothes off of the rack and to style her own hair.

With her sister, Edythe, Coretta attended a class reunion at Lincoln High School in Marion in 1996. Both of the sisters enjoyed seeing former teachers and classmates, and they spent time at their old home. "We were like little girls again," Edythe noted. "We talked all night, we ran the house, we went to the reunion. It felt so good to be home and with the family. I'm looking forward to more times like these."[4] Coretta agreed. She closed the interview by adding, "It takes time [to slow down], but I am getting there."[5]

Around the time of her retirement, Coretta also had increasing responsibilities related to the care of her own aging parents. Her mother, Bernice, died at age 91 of Alzheimer's disease in an Atlanta nursing home in February 1996. Her father continued to live in Marion. He had served on the county school board during the 1980s, and he ran his store until he was 91. He died in 1999 at age 99.

Coretta also continued to live in her home at 234 Sunset, alone except for her assistant who came during the day. Her children and friends were concerned about her, as the neighborhood had become home to more problems related to drugs and other criminal activities. In 1996, someone broke into her home while she was asleep. The police captured the burglar when he used a two-way radio that he had stolen, which was connected to the security at the King Center. He was charged with the break-in and several other violent acts in the neighborhood. He told police that he had debated killing Coretta but stopped when he saw a photo of Martin in the bedroom. This incident caused the children and friends to be even more concerned and to look for a safer living arrangement for their mother. They initiated conversations with the National Park Service about buying the home as an addition to the historic site, but they did not reach an agreement that was acceptable to all concerned.

The King Family also explored possibilities for the National Park Service to purchase the King Center property. In March 1999, the Park Service leased the historic Ebenezer Baptist Church sanctuary, where Martin and his father preached. The church moved into a larger facility across the street, next to the King site visitors' center, called the Horizon Sanctuary. Dexter noted that the King Center would not give up its mission of promoting nonviolence, even if they gave up responsibility for maintaining the physical complex.

In the aftermath of the dispute with the National Park Service and the controversy over the King Estate's handling of the King papers, the government did not appropriate funds to purchase the King Center. In addition, a dispute arose between the children, with Dexter and Yolanda in favor of selling the Center and Martin III and Bernice opposed to selling it.

HONORING CORETTA FOR HER WORK

Bernice presided over the 2000 King Holiday commemorative service. In a preaching voice reminiscent of her father's, she brought the crowd to its feet multiple times, calling for all those present to accept their call and assignment for life. Bernice also offered a strong defense of her mother when she introduced her to speak: "She is not worthy of the criticism she has received, and unless you have cried like she has, had to raise four children without a husband, with little or no money, then you don't know . . . So I say to my brothers and sisters, leave my mama alone."[6] When Coretta began her speech, she joked that she could take care of herself, but she then shifted into the realm of politics, suggesting that African Americans had seen important political, social, and economic gains under the Clinton-Gore administration. Vice President Al Gore was the keynote speaker for the service, and he used it to announce a matching federal and private appropriation for the restoration of Ebenezer Church.

Later in 2000, Coretta joined with the National Park Service and former President Jimmy Carter to mark the 20th anniversary of the Martin Luther King, Jr. Historic District. More than 500 people attended the ceremony, which honored President Carter, Christine Farris, John Lewis, and Coretta. Coretta reflected on the site, "I think we all knew at the time that something beautiful and important was being born here on Auburn Avenue . . . a precious historical treasure for the nation and the world."[7]

The next couple of years Coretta stayed out of the limelight on the whole. She continued to make appearances at the King Center occasionally, providing a highlight for visitors to the site. Television writer Tina Andrews began to work on a miniseries about her life, with the proposed title "Coretta Scott King: The Woman Beside the Man," and she visited Atlanta to shadow Coretta during the King Holiday festivities. The miniseries remained unfinished at the time of Coretta's death.

Coretta continued to make statements about areas of concern, deriving her arguments from her interpretation of Martin's philosophy. At a service of remembrance in April 2001, Coretta stated, "Today we call on Martin's followers all over the world to begin mobilizing for a new season of service in the spirit of nonviolence. We call on you to educate the children in the methods of nonviolence; we call you to take a stand against poverty and homelessness, to speak out against racism, anti-Semitism, homophobia, and all forms of bigotry; we call you to protest against the death penalty and racial profiling."[8]

While she was no longer the chairman and CEO of the King Center, Coretta continued to try to avoid positions that would place the King Center in a negative light. In 2002, First Lady Laura Bush attended the King Holiday commemorative service. Coretta did not talk to her about her views on the war in Afghanistan, which had just begun, yet, the same week, she had spoken to the *Atlanta Journal-Constitution* about her life-long commitment to pacifism. "In his [Martin's] last years, he said, 'If I am the only person left who believes in nonviolence, I will be that sole person calling for nonviolence. And I will stand with that for the rest of my days.' I, too, share that conviction."[9]

During the service, she misintroduced Laura Bush as Barbara Bush. She corrected herself, as the crowd laughed, "Her mother-in-law was very dear to me."

Calls for peace continued to dominate King Holiday services, while the wars in Afghanistan and Iraq continued. In 2004, President George W. Bush indicated that he would like to visit and place a wreath on Martin's tomb. Some planners of the King Holiday March protested that he had invited himself and that required security precautions would interfere with their planned march. However, a compromise was reached, and President Bush did visit the tomb after a brief visit with Coretta.

FAMILY DISAGREEMENTS

As Coretta's children took public stands of their own on issues, their views occasionally clashed with those of Coretta's. One issue where their differences played out in the media was gay rights.

At the time of the King Holiday in 2002, an article in the *Atlanta Constitution* pointed out that this was a holiday held in high esteem by gay people. The article noted that Coretta "has always been supportive of gay issues and has been a consistent champion of gay rights."[10] The article noted that gay activists have been inspired by Martin's teachings and have compared their struggle to that of the civil rights movement. They pointed out that Martin had worked closely with Bayard Rustin, a gay man, even entrusting to him the behind-the-scenes work for the 1963 March on Washington.

In 2004, when Congress was considering a Constitutional amendment to outlaw gay marriage, Coretta spoke at a rally in New Jersey, noting that gay marriage was a civil rights issue. This claim of connection by gay rights activists did not sit well with other civil rights veterans, especially those aligned closely with fundamentalist Christian churches. In December 2004, Bernice participated in a march sponsored by her church New Birth Missionary Baptist Church and led by its pastor Bishop Eddie Long. The march began at the King Center, with Bernice lighting a torch from the eternal flame in honor of Martin and passing it to Bishop Long. The goals of the march were multiple, but one of them was support for a proposed Constitutional ban on gay marriage. Bishop Long noted that the goal was "to present a unified vision of righteousness and justice."[11] Coretta did not speak out directly against the march, although she had noted that "constitutional amendments should be used to expand freedom, not restrict it."[12] On the other hand, Bernice noted at a sermon in New Zealand, "I know deep down in my sanctified soul that he [Martin] did not take a bullet for same-sex unions."[13]

FAMILY GOOD TIMES

However, there were other topics on which Coretta and the children continued to agree in their interpretation of history. For Coretta's 75th birthday celebration, Yolanda organized a full weekend of activities, from Friday evening at the theater, to a Saturday afternoon cruise on the Stone Mountain Park riverboat, to dinner at Paschal's Restaurant, and Sunday morning church at Ebenezer Baptist. Yolanda noted the symbolism of the party taking place at Stone Mountain, as the mountain had been used for Ku Klux Klan rallies in Martin's day. "As I child I remember being told you cannot go there, particularly at night, because it was dangerous. And for us to be able . . . to leisurely float around the mountain, I think, is such an appropriate tribute to how far we have come and the fact that she's contributed so much to that."[14]

In May of 2003, Coretta appeared on the Oprah Winfrey Show after having received an "age defying makeover." Oprah's stylist had cut her hair, which was the first professional cut she had had in 20 years. A make-up artist suggested techniques for making her complexion look brighter, noting that Coretta had been making the mistake that many older women make of using too much foundation. He also reshaped her eyebrows. Designers found an outfit that made her appear thinner and taller. Oprah raved over the transformation. Coretta smiled but didn't elaborate on her feelings about the makeover.

Also in fall 2003, Coretta finally moved out of her home on Sunset Avenue. Her new home was a penthouse condominium in a high rise in Buckhead (an Atlanta neighborhood). The building featured round-the-clock security, and it was also home to the Atlanta condos of Elton John and Janet Jackson. The home was "an anonymous gift," although many people suspected that it was made by Oprah Winfrey because her designer was seen in the building about the time of Coretta's move. In addition, the *Chicago Defender* reported the story in January 2005, although they did not cite their source. The "Peach Buzz" column of the *Atlanta Constitution* checked court records and reported that the warranty deed was made by Overground Railroad LLC, the same entity that purchased a condo in Chicago where Oprah Winfrey's mother lives.

In June 2004, Coretta returned to the Antioch College campus for a reunion and to celebrate the 150th anniversary of the college's founding. The college presented her the Horace Mann Award, named after the founding president. Coretta spoke to the students, faculty, and alumni who were present. Yolanda, Martin III, and Bernice accompanied her, as well as two staff people from the King Center.

Coretta's speech reflected on the ways in which the Antioch experience had affected her life and work. She proudly acknowledged the college's emphasis on student service, as well as its curriculum that fostered critical thinking. In addition, she traced the school's history of racial inclusion and its commitment to broader diversity, which she defined as "students and faculty of various religious, ethnic, and age groups should be well-represented on campus. The same is true for gay and lesbian people, people with disabilities, and people from low-income families. The university should look like America—a vibrant multi-cultural mosaic."[15]

Coretta also called those in attendance to action and urged that they vote. She identified a range of national and international issues in which she wanted to see reform—from gun control to health care, from education funding to job training, from an end to the war in Iraq to the cancellation of the debts of poor countries in Africa. She also called for an increase in the number of women in elected and other leadership positions.

She tied all of these issues together and suggested that change would emerge out of nonviolence. "What we most desperately need in our world today is a new nonviolent revolution, a revolution to provide hope and opportunity for disadvantaged people; a revolution that is set on eradicating racism, sexism, homophobia, xenophobia, and all forms of prejudice, bigotry, and discrimination; a revolution that embraces justices, peace, sisterhood and brotherhood."[16] It was a powerful speech and a reiteration of beliefs that had been important to her throughout her life.

UNRESOLVED ISSUE: THE KING CENTER

In January 2004, Dexter resigned as president, CEO, and chairman of the King Center. Martin III assumed the positions of president and CEO, stepping down from the leadership of the SCLC. Coretta agreed to resume the position of chairman of the board on a temporary basis. Dexter had been living in Malibu, California, since 2000, and the resignation enabled him to stop commuting. King Center observers suggested that the ascension of Martin III as leader would mean that the King Center would increase its focus on social justice activism, an area of work that had not been emphasized during the era of Dexter's leadership.

However, in early 2005, reports hit the media that the King Center's facilities were crumbling and in need of $12 million in maintenance and repairs. At the same time, Martin III and Dexter were both paid six-figure salaries. The staff, which had included a total of 71 people in 1986, was reduced to 22, with most of those employed to work in the gift shop. The board of directors had also been reduced in size, from a high of 150 that included a "who's who" of Black America, down to 8 family members and Andrew Young. Andrew Young responded and called for the federal government to assist with the maintenance needs, but the government did not move in that direction. Another newspaper article questioned the payment of large sums to for-profit IPM, which was also run by Dexter, by the nonprofit King Center. Coretta did not comment in any of these articles. Dexter noted that the payments to IPM were to support staff work by IPM employees who devoted time to performing licensing tasks for the Center.

CORETTA'S LAST INTERVIEW

In conjunction with the King Holiday in 2005, Coretta participated in an interview with journalist Tavis Smiley for his syndicated public broadcasting program. They taped the interview in Ebenezer Baptist Church, and it would be her final public interview. Bernice attended with her mother.

Smiley asked Coretta to reflect on what it meant to her to walk into that setting. She cited a variety of memories, from singing in the choir to listening to Martin preach eloquent sermons that had become famous. "And all of the wonderful people who visited this church over the years and spoke here, but the wonderful membership who gave us so much love and support, because there was always something happening in our lives that we needed to have support for."[17] Her acknowledgement of the role of the congregation was poignant, partly because Coretta was in the midst of another time in which she needed community support.

Smiley then asked her about Kingian nonviolence and whether it was applicable to the contemporary world. To this question, Coretta gave a passionate response, "It will work today, 2000 years from now, 5000. Yes, absolutely."[18] Smiley asked about Osama Bin Laden. Coretta replied, "If Martin's philosophy had been embraced and lived out in Iraq and other places, we wouldn't have Bin Laden." She spoke eloquently about nonviolence as a process that needs to be developed over time. She added that she wished for the King Center to teach nonviolence to students from preschool, through twelve grades, to college, and to adults in the working world.

The interview shifted gears. Smiley asked Coretta to reflect on personal interactions with Martin. She talked about how he would get depressed and disappointed occasionally, and she would help him through saying positive things. Coretta asserted that she knew Martin as she had spent more time with him than anyone else during his adult life. She had witnessed his commitment to follow his conscience, to serve God and to serve mankind. She noted that Martin put those efforts first, even ahead of mundane issues such as defending himself when he was falsely accused of wrongdoing.

Then the interview took a humorous turn. Tavis Smiley asked Coretta why she had never married again? She turned the tables on him, noting that he, too, was unmarried. After some laughter and Smiley squirming, Coretta explained that she had married a cause when she married Martin, and her commitment to that cause remained first even after his death. But she also indicated how her vision had emerged from the cause:

> So when Martin was no longer here, you know, it was like, "I will do whatever I can, God, to continue in my own way. I don't have Martin Luther King, Jr.'s abilities and skills, but I do have skills that you have given me and I will use those to the best of my ability, and I need to know the direction." It took a while for me to get the direction. And I really felt that it finally—it came through as being the King Center—to develop—to take, not only just helping, but I had to get in there and lead it myself. And it was my vision, and that I had to—whatever it took. But my children were always my first priority.[19]

ILLNESS STRIKES

A few months after this interview, Coretta fell ill. She went to Piedmont Hospital for an irregular heart-beat on April 26, 2005. Medical professionals stabilized her and released her with medication to control the problem. Four months later, she had a stroke. She remained in the hospital for several weeks, and then she went to a holistic rehabilitation facility for additional treatment.

A dispute regarding control of the King Center hit the media on September 30, 2005. While Dexter had given up the CEO position to his brother, he had retained the title of board chairman and chief operating officer. While Martin concentrated on giving speeches, fundraising, and ceremonial functions, Dexter continued to run staff meetings via speaker phone from his home in California. The two brothers were not communicating with each other. At the heart of the issue was the question of direction of the Center—would it concentrate on management of the Estate and the packaging of Martin's intellectual property, or would it focus on social justice activities? As Coretta was still recuperating, she was unable to intervene and rectify the situation.

In December 2005, the King Center board voted Isaac Farris, Jr., Coretta's nephew, as president and CEO. Martin III remained on the board, but he noted to the media that he would concentrate on taking care of Coretta. With Dexter's encouragement, the King Center board began to consider the sale of the King Center property, Coretta's home on Sunset Avenue, and Martin's papers that were part of the King Center collection.

Andrew Young suggested that the family dispute had been resolved and that "Coretta understood that one day the center would be turned over to the Park Service."[20] He added that the sale would allow the King family to concentrate on the King legacy rather than maintaining property.

Yet, Martin King III was not ready to agree to the sale, noting "that there are quite a number of outstanding issues pertaining to the proposed strategy that have not been resolved."[21] While his top priority remained the care of Coretta, he remained committed to the King Center as a "robust, programmatic structure." He announced that he was also exploring other options for continuing the work outside of the King Center structure.

Isaac Farris indicated that his vision for the King Center was that it be like a think-tank. He suggested that the center had lost its way due to attempts to serve too many programs and constituencies.

Coretta made her last public appearance as part of the Salute to Greatness fundraiser for the King Center on January 14, 2006. She electrified the ballroom when she appeared in a wheel chair, accompanied by Bernice. She stood briefly and received a standing ovation, but she was unable to speak. Isaac Farris spoke after her appearance, assuring the audience that the mission and work of the King Center would continue, even if the physical complex was sold. He indicated that an announcement about the disposition of the Center was forthcoming.

However, the next public statements were conflicting. On January 16, 2006, Dexter announced that Coretta was in favor of the sale.

> The thing that people don't know is that from the beginning the National Park Service has envisioned buying this property. This is not something new. My mother finally agreed that it made sense. One of her greatest regrets was that she did not provide an endowment for the center when she was younger and had the energy to do that. She doesn't have the energy for that now. This sale would provide an endowment.[22]

On the same day, Bernice and Martin III coauthored an opinion piece in the *Atlanta Constitution* where they announced their intention that "the King Center is both a physical memorial (the facilities along with our father's tomb) and a living legacy (the programs for justice, equality, and community) and that they are spiritually indivisible. We believe that selling the memorial will compromise the legacy."[23] While they were not opposed to governmental involvement, they insisted that the King Center remain independent so that its voice not be compromised by governmental control. They also added that they were primarily concerned with assisting their mother during her illness.

Coretta's health did not improve. Though she checked in to seek treatments at a holistic health center in Mexico, just across the border from San Diego, she died on January 30, 2006. The family announced that she had been suffering from ovarian cancer, as well as the after-effects of the stroke. She had checked into the facility under an assumed name, though accompanied by Bernice, so that she could have privacy. Andrew Young noted, "They [the family] felt that their mother had lived a totally public life and they wanted to spend some private time with her and they didn't want the public to intrude."[24]

NOTES

1. Russ Devault, "Stars to Turn out for Tribute to Mrs. King," *Atlanta Constitution*, April 27, 1993, D-1.

2. Sonia Murray, "Through You . . . We Remember," *Atlanta Constitution*, May 1, 1993, B-12.

3. John Blake, "King Center Torch Passes," *Atlanta Constitution*, January 16, 1995 A6.

4. Hollis R. Towns, "Capturing Her Dreams," *Atlanta Constitution*, July 21, 1996, M3.

5. Ibid.

6. Ernie Suggs, "$1 Million Provided to Restore Church," *Atlanta Constitution*, January 17, 2000, A1, A8.

7. Ernie Suggs, "MLK Site Hailed as Source of Hope," *Atlanta Constitution*, October 19, 2000, D-1.

8. Hervey Pean, "Continue King's Work Family Urges Gathering," *Atlanta Constitution*, April 12, 2001, D-3.

9. Mae Gentry, "In the Words of Coretta King," *Atlanta Constitution*, January 20, 2002, C8.

10. Charles Yoo, "Gays Hold Holiday in High Esteem," *Atlanta Constitution*, January 21, 2002, D3.

11. John Blake, "March Divides King Followers," *Atlanta Constitution*, December 11, 2004, A12.

12. Ibid.

13. Ibid.

14. Mae Gentry, "Coretta King Celebrated 75th by Keeping Busy," *Atlanta Constitution*, April 28, 2002, C3.

15. "Address by Coretta Scott King, Antioch Reunion 2004," http://www.antioch-college.edu/news/csk/2004Mannacceptance.html.

16. Ibid.

17. Tavis Smiley, "Interview with Coretta Scott King," original air date January 17, 2005, http://www.pbs.org/kcet/tavissmiley/archive/200501/20050117_king.html.

18. Ibid.

19. Ibid.

20. Maria Saporta and Ernie Suggs, "Board of Landmark Weighs Sale to Park Service, Signaling Shift in Power Struggle over its Future," *Atlanta Constitution*, December 23, 2005, A-10.

21. Ibid.

22. Jeffry Scott and Christopher Quinn, "Dexter King Says Mother Backs Sale," *Atlanta Constitution*, January 16, 2006, B1-B2.

23. Bernice King and Martin Luther King III, "Protecting Noble Vision," *Atlanta Constitution*, January 16, 2006, A15.

24. Mae Gentry, Bob Keefe, and Maria Saporta, "Matriarch Had Sought Treatment for Cancer," *Atlanta Constitution*, February 1, 2006, A10.

Chapter 14

HOMEGOING SERVICES

The announcement of Coretta's death caught the media by surprise, but they quickly moved into action developing and sharing retrospectives about her life and work. In Atlanta, mourners and journalists gathered at Martin's crypt at the King Center to share their grief and leave mementos. Poet (and family friend) Maya Angelou noted on ABC's *Good Morning America* show, "It's a bleak morning for me and for many people. Yet it's a great morning because we have a chance to look at her and see what she did and who she was."[1]

For Atlanta journalists, many of whom knew Coretta personally, it was a difficult story to cover. V-103 Radio's morning show host Frank Ski noted, "You're trying to be a journalist, but it's like a family member passing." WSB television's longtime anchor woman Monica Kaufman referred to Coretta as "Corey" during an interview.[2]

Bishop Eddie Long provided a jet to take Martin III to California to meet Bernice, Dexter, and Yolanda and to bring Coretta's body back to Atlanta. Atlanta Mayor Shirley Franklin and Georgia Governor Sonny Perdue reached out to the family and offered assistance with funeral logistics.

The family announced funeral arrangements on February 3. In accordance with Coretta's strong desire, plans were made for her to be buried adjacent to Martin at the King Center.

Portions of Coretta's funeral arrangements echoed Martin's, but there were also many differences, some of which demonstrated changes that had come about in Atlanta and American society in the 40 years since Martin's death. Whereas Governor Lester Maddox closed the Capitol on the day of Martin's service and posted guards to keep the mourners off of the grounds, Governor Sonny Perdue invited the family to have Coretta's body lay in state in the Capitol rotunda. The tribute at the Capitol made her the first woman and the first African American to receive such an honor.

Coretta's coffin was carried from place to place in a silver, black lacquer, and glass carriage drawn by horses, in contrast with the rough hewn wagon and mule team that carried Martin's coffin. The funeral home employees wore top hats and formal suits, whereas some SCLC staffers had worn overalls to Martin's service.

At least 42,000 visitors paid their respects at the Capitol. An additional 100,000 stood in line in the cold and rain to pay their respects in the historic Ebenezer Baptist Church sanctuary where Coretta's body lay in repose on February 6. That same day, a variety of performers, including Oprah Winfrey and Gladys Knight, participated in a musical tribute in the new Horizon Sanctuary of Ebenezer.

The funeral service was at New Birth Missionary Baptist Church in the south part of DeKalb County. New Birth's sanctuary seated 10,000 people. The family recognized that despite the central role that Ebenezer had played in their mother's lives, Ebenezer was simply too small to contain the variety of family members, dignitaries, and other friends who wanted to participate in this program. Also, Bernice was on staff at New Birth.

President George W. Bush attended and spoke, as did former Presidents Jimmy Carter, George H. W. Bush, and Bill Clinton. The first lady of South Africa, Zanela Mbeki, offered remarks. In addition, a contingent of U.S. Senators and Representatives attended, and Representative John Conyers and Senator Edward Kennedy spoke.

There were tributes from the ranks of the civil and human rights community, including Joseph Lowery, president emeritus of the SCLC, and Dorothy Height of the National Council of Negro Women. Former participants in King Center programs spoke, including Charles Rachael, who gave up membership in the Crips gang as a result of training that he received in nonviolence. Close friends and family, including the daughters of Ralph Abernathy and Malcolm X, spoke. A variety of representatives of the faith community also paid tribute, including Bishop T. D. Jakes and Dr. Robert Schuler. The final tributes were by Maya Angelou and Andrew Young, and Bernice King offered the eulogy.

Musicians Michael Bolton, Bebe Winans, Stevie Wonder, and CeCe Winans performed, as well as the Total Praise Choir of New Birth, the Martin Luther King, Jr. Commemorative Chorus, and the Atlanta Symphony. In recognition of Coretta's classical music training, Juandalynn Abernathy, a soprano, sang the aria "Vissi d'Arte, Vissi d'Amore" from Puccini's *Tosca*. Other musical selections ranged from the spiritual "Ain't Got Time to Die," to the gospel hymn "His Eye Is on the Sparrow," to contemporary anthems "Total Praise" and "Stand."

The service recessional was the "Hallelujah Chorus" from Handel's *Messiah*, a selection that was always included in the annual King Holiday commemorative services. One song that was not included was "We Shall Overcome," which was always the final song of the commemorative services.

Some of the speakers interjected political commentary into their remarks. Perhaps the most pointed example was when Joseph Lowery asserted, "We now know there were no weapons of mass destruction . . . but Coretta knew and we know that there are weapons of misdirection right here. Millions without health insurance, poverty abound. For war billions more, but no more for the poor."[3] Attendees observed that this was a jab at President George W. Bush. Later on in the program, when former President George H. W. Bush spoke, he tried to make light of the criticism, noting that it was in keeping with a tradition of verbal sparring between Lowery and him that dated back to his own tenure in the White House.

Former President Bill Clinton took a different approach. Looking at the example of Coretta's life, he asked attendees, "What are you going to do with the rest of your life?" He also directed a special question at Atlanta—"What is your responsibility for the future of the King Center?"[4] noting that Atlanta is home to many successful businesses and wealthy African Americans.

In all, the service lasted eight hours long. After the funeral, the family participated in a private burial at the King Center. Like Martin, Coretta was first placed in a temporary mausoleum until Martin's crypt could be adjusted to house her coffin. The family dedicated a new double crypt on November 20, 2006.

Coretta's will was filed in Fulton County Probate Court in May 2006. This will had been drawn up in 1976, at which point all of her children were under 21. Originally, Edythe Bagley and Christine Farris were to be executors and caretakers of the King Children. However, Coretta had amended her will to make Yolanda executor in 1984. She bequeathed $5,000 to the King Center and $5,000 to Ebenezer Baptist Church. She also left $10,000 each to her brother and sister and to Christine Farris. The will did not include details about the family's financial worth or the value of Martin's estate, via which his intellectual property was managed.

PUBLIC TRIBUTES

During 2007, Atlantans began to plan for ways to pay tribute to Coretta's memory. The Salute to Greatness fundraiser was in her memory and in honor of the King papers Atlanta initiative, which had begun in summer 2006. Bernice King donated funds to her alma mater, Spelman College, to establish a scholarship in her mother's memory. In addition, the Atlanta Public Schools set up the Coretta Scott King Leadership Academy for middle school girls.

During the 2007 legislative session, a bill was introduced to mount a portrait of Coretta in the state capitol. Similar bills had also been mounted to honor other African American women, including Rosa Parks. Ultimately, the bills were tabled, and the legislature set up a Study Committee on Capitol Art to determine policies about criteria for mounting portraits, based on the limited amount of wall space available.

MORE UNEXPECTED TRAGEDY, THEN JOY

Yolanda King died suddenly and tragically in May 2007. She suffered a heart attack in her home state of California. Her memorial service took place in Ebenezer Baptist Church, and it also attracted many mourners. For the second time in less than 18 months, Martin III, Dexter, and Bernice gathered for the homegoing of a beloved family member.

In September 2007, journalists from KHOU television station in Houston broke the story that the FBI had continued to spy on Coretta after Martin's death. Through Freedom of Information Act inquiries, Mark Greenblatt and David Raziq obtained Coretta's FBI file, which included around 500 pages of information. Though some of the documents were partially or completely censored, the file noted that the FBI began to closely track Coretta's comings and goings after Martin's death. Agents also intercepted letters and they read her memoir *My Life with Martin Luther King, Jr.*, in search of signs of subversive activities. One FBI agent noted that Coretta's "selfless, magnanimous, decorous attitude is belied by [her] actual shrewd, calculating, businesslike activities."[5]

What the FBI was concerned about was that Coretta would make connections between the growing anti-Vietnam movement and the civil rights movement. Some documents noted that White House officials were briefed on items that had been observed about Coretta. They also noted a counter-intelligence effort against Ralph Abernathy, by which agents sought to establish rapport with him via warning him about supposed threats on his life. The surveillance stopped in 1972 upon the death of Director J. Edgar Hoover. The contemporary FBI declined to comment, except to note that their agency's practices have changed.

The journalists who broke the story shared the documents with Isaac Farris, Jr. and the King Center. He noted, "Here was a woman who was trying to be supportive to her husband. Raise their four kids and continue on in his footsteps. It just shows what a sad and tragic period we were going through during the 1960s."[6]

The 2008 Salute to Greatness dinner was a happier occasion, in that Martin III announced his marriage (which had actually occurred around the time of Coretta's death). In addition, the couple was expecting a baby. Yolanda Renee King, the first grandchild of Martin and Coretta, was born on May 25, 2008.

NOTES

1. Mae Gentry, Bob Keefe, and Maria Saporta, "Matriarch Had Sought Treatment for Cancer," *Atlanta Constitution*, February 1, 2006, A10

2. Phil Kloer and Rodney Ho, "Local National News Organizations Spring to Action," *Atlanta Journal Constitution*, February 1, 2006, A14

3. Bill Torpy and Maria Saporta, "Political Jabs Pepper Funeral Oratory," *Atlanta Journal-Constitution*, February 8, 2006, A6.

4. Maria Saporta and Craig Schneider, "Clinton Challenges Atlantans," *Atlanta Journal-Constitution*, February 8, 2006, A6

5. "11 News Exclusive: Inside the FBI's Secret Files on Coretta Scott King," September 1, 2007, http://www.khou.com/topstories/stories/khou070830_ac_scottkingfiles.85364faa.html.

6. Ibid.

Chapter 15

THE CORETTA SCOTT KING
BOOK AWARDS

In 1969, two school librarians, Mabel McKissick of Connecticut and Glyndon Greer of New Jersey, had a conversation in the exhibit hall during the American Library Association (ALA) conference in Atlantic City. They noted that no African American author or illustrator had yet been selected to receive the Newberry or Caldecott Medals (the major awards for achievement in children's literature). Publisher John M. Carroll, overhearing their lament, suggested, "Why don't you ladies start an award to do just that?"[1]

Greer and McKissick pursued the idea and sought assistance from other librarians in the New Jersey area. John M. Carroll agreed to underwrite the cost of a plaque. Glyndon Greer suggested that the awards be named in honor of Coretta Scott King, a friend of hers, and that the awards "commemorate the life and work of Martin Luther King, Jr. and honor his wife for her courage and determination in continuing the work for peace and brotherhood."[2] Greer requested to Coretta that she allow the use of her name, and Coretta agreed, but she was not otherwise involved in establishing the program.

During the May 1970 meeting of the New Jersey Library Association, they presented the first award to Lillie Patterson for her biography *Martin Luther King, Jr.: Man of Peace*. Garrard Publishing Company provided complimentary copies of the winning book to attendees. In conjunction with the presentation, they invited Sylvia Drew, the daughter of pioneering physician Charles Drew, to speak.

At the summer 1970 ALA conference, they organized a session to represent the award and to call attention to the book, but the program was not yet affiliated formally with the ALA.

Recognizing value and success in their initial effort, the founders reached out to colleagues in the African American library and education networks around the country. They solicited and gained involvement from leaders from Atlanta, New York, and California. They also identified a contact at Johnson Publishing Company of Chicago, who began to provide a cash award to the recipient. Their initial contacts were primarily the result of word of mouth, yet as they were working on a topic that was of concern to an increasing number of professionals, they quickly found allies in their effort.

The awards breakfast occurred for the first time in 1972, during the ALA conference. In 1974, the group presented the award to an illustrator for the first time, George Ford, for his drawings in Sharon Bell Mathis' biography *Ray Charles*.

Also in 1974, the awards committee commissioned Lev Mills, chairman of the Art Department at Atlanta University, to create a seal to go on recipient books, following the practice of the Newberry and Caldecott Medals. Organizers recognized that having a visual symbol on recipient awards would assist in raising the visibility and significance of the awards. Mills' symbol includes a circle with the words "peace," "nonviolent social change," "brotherhood," and "Coretta Scott King Award" on it. Inside the circle is a dove that symbolizes peace. Below the dove is a pyramid that encloses a child reading a book, and below the book are symbols of the major world faith traditions. The seals for winning books are produced in bronze, symbolizing African skin tones, and the seals for honor books (runners-up) are produced in silver.

In 1980, the task force that organized the awards aligned with the Social Responsibilities Round Table of the ALA. Glyndon Greer served as the first chair until her death in August of that year. In 1982, the ALA Council adopted the Coretta Scott King Award as an official part of their awards program. The awards breakfast became a highlight of the ALA conferences with approximately 500 to 800 people attending annually.

The ALA affiliation provided additional publicity for the program as well as administrative support for organizing the breakfast. With the ALA, the award sought additional support from corporate and individual donors. The Coca-Cola Bottling Company came on board as well as Famous Amos Cookies. In 1980, *Encyclopedia Brittanica* began to provide sets to the winning authors, and *World Book* did the same for the winning illustrators. In 1989, the ALA published the first full-color brochure to highlight the program and solicit nominations.

Through the leadership and activism of the library community, the number of children's books by African American authors and illustrators increased. In the face of this proliferation, the awards committee refined their criteria and set up a jury process to select winners. In 1993, they established the Genesis Award to recognize a young author or illustrator whose material shows great promise. The name of this award was later changed to the John Steptoe Award for New Talent.

In 1990, the host committee for the breakfast began the practice of inviting a group of local children to attend. These children would receive copies of the award books as well as other mementos. Their participation reminded the adults of the purpose of the award—to promote an understanding and appreciation of the culture and contributions of all people to the American dream.

The ALA also established another outreach from the awards via the Review Book Donation Grants. Annually, after-school programs, family literacy projects, homeless shelters, and underfunded schools and public libraries can apply to receive sets of the books under consideration for awards. Grants enable these programs to increase the number of high-quality materials in their collection.

In 1998, the name of the ALA committee that handled the awards changed to the Ethnic and Multicultural Information Exchange Round Table (EMIERT). As the volume of recipient books reached 175, the leaders of EMIERT recognized the body of awardees as an important research collection in the history of African American children's literature, and they sought to raise funds for endowed collections. While they did not yet identify a permanent home for the collection, they did place sets in public libraries in Atlanta and at Alabama A&M University. They also began to market bookmarks about the awards program as a fundraising vehicle that promoted public awareness of the program.

The award books were in a variety of formats and on a variety of topics. Some were biographies or historical fiction; others depicted contemporary social situations and themes. They were aimed at readers of a variety of ages, from preschool to high school. Some books were drama or poetry. There were several repeat recipients, including author Walter Dean Myers and illustrator Ashley Bryan.

Neither Coretta nor the King Center was involved in the administration of the program or the selection of award books, but Coretta did attend the awards breakfast in 1984, 1993, and 2002. Yolanda also attended and spoke in 1989.

In 1999, in an interview with the *Dallas Morning News*, Coretta noted, "When you teach young people love and values and how to be peaceful and respectful in your disagreements, that people have more in common than they are different, I think they will learn to like people and respect people who are different from themselves."[3] That is the motivation which led Coretta to loan her name to the Coretta Scott King Awards, which constitute another of her legacies. Upon Coretta's death, Fran Ware, the chair of the awards committee, noted, "These books represent the values we know children need to be well-equipped in the world as adults, valued like love and truth and peace and sharing and happiness and honesty."[4] Into the future, as children and parents and teachers read books with the Coretta Scott King Award seal, they will be learning things that Coretta wanted them to learn.

NOTES

1. Henrietta M. Smith, ed., *The Coretta Scott King Awards from Vision to Reality* (Chicago and London: The American Library Association, 1994), ix.

2. Ibid.

3. "The Coretta Scott King Award News," February 1, 2006, http://www.ala.org/ala/emiert/corettascottkingbookaward/abouttheawarda/awardnews/csknews.html.

4. Ibid.

CONCLUSION

Like all people, Coretta Scott King lived in the midst of times, events, and places that affected her life. From Perry County, Alabama, to Yellow Springs, Ohio (home of Antioch College); from Montgomery to Atlanta; from Washington, D.C., to around the world, Coretta interacted with and influenced a variety of people who shaped and influenced her in their turn. At the same time, Coretta was a visionary and leader who worked toward change and making the world a better place. She was both of her times and ahead of her times.

Through her marriage and partnership with Martin Luther King, Jr., she was part of the struggle to obtain civil rights for African Americans in the United States. After his death, she helped shape the memory of Martin and the civil rights movement, even as she continued to advance efforts toward fulfilling the portions of the effort that she saw as unfulfilled.

Her efforts kept her busy and required her to juggle multiple duties. She also had to find ways to negotiate between political and economic realities and the ideals that she was aiming to accomplish. Because she was holistic in her thinking, she didn't see her various stands and acts as contradictory or in irreconcilable conflict. Similar to her father's experiences during segregation, when he confidently looked white oppressors in the eye, Coretta sought to negotiate through a position of strength, regardless of whether she was in fact in a position of power. The strength came from her convictions and faith that she was working toward the right. The strength also manifested the power of nonviolence.

In her autobiography, Coretta explained the core of her convictions: "I believe that there is a plan and a purpose for each person's life and that there are forces working in the universe to bring about good and to create a community of love and brotherhood. Those who can attune themselves to these forces—to God's purpose—can become special instruments of His will."[1] Throughout her life, Coretta saw herself as being in tune with these greater purposes.

With her family and close friends, she was thoughtful and warm and had a dry sense of humor. In the public eye, on the other hand, she was calm and stoic, even aloof. She sometimes seemed so wrapped up in accomplishing her purpose that she cut herself off from the community around her. But all of these aspects of character contributed to who Coretta Scott King was.

Coretta raised and was a strong influence on her children. However, the children also clearly grew up in a different time and space than the one in which she was rooted. They and others of their generation are the beneficiaries of the political struggle for freedom that Coretta and Martin endured. Time will tell how they ultimately determine to resolve the fate of the King Center's facilities and what its ongoing purposes will be.

In addition, time will tell about the impact of Coretta Scott King on history. The organizing and opening of Coretta's personal papers in the King Center archive will help future scholars understand her more fully.

In the meantime, her close friend Andrew Young gets the final word, "she lived a graceful and beautiful life"[2]—one that inspired and set a standard that people unknown to her and generations yet to come will reflect on and admire.

NOTES

1. Ernie Suggs, "She's at Peace Now," *Atlanta Journal-Constitution*, February 1, 2006, A13.

2. Ibid, A12.

SELECTED RESOURCES

MEMOIRS

King, Coretta Scott. *My Life with Martin Luther King, Jr.* New York: Holt, Rinehart, Winston, 1969.

King, Dexter Scott. *Growing Up King: An Intimate Memoir.* New York: Warner Books, 2003.

HISTORIC SITES

Alabama Historic Marker, Scott Family Home, Highway 29 North, Perry County, Alabama (home and store not open to the public).

Coretta Scott King Monument, Mt. Tabor African Methodist Episcopal-Zion Church, Highway 29 North, Perry County, Alabama.

Dexter Parsonage Museum, 309 S. Jackson Street, Montgomery, Alabama.

"The King Room," Freedom Hall, The Martin Luther King, Jr. Center for Nonviolent Social Change, 449 Auburn Avenue, Atlanta, Georgia.

BOOKS

Albert, Peter J., and Ronald Hoffman. *We Shall Overcome: Martin Luther King, Jr. and the Black Freedom Struggle.* New York: Pantheon Books, 1990.

Branch, Taylor. *At Canaan's Edge: America in the King Years, 1965–68.* New York: Simon and Schuster, 2006.

Branch, Taylor. *Parting the Waters: America in the King Years, 1954–63.* New York: Simon and Schuster, 1988.

Branch, Taylor. *Pillar of Fire: America in the King Years, 1963–65*. New York: Simon and Schuster, 1998.

Garrow, David. *Bearing the Cross: Martin Luther King, Jr., and the Southern Christian Leadership Conference*. New York: Harper Collins, 1986.

Vivian, Octavia. *Coretta: The Story of Coretta Scott King*. Minneapolis: Fortress Press, 2006.

ESSAY

Crawford, Vicki. "Coretta Scott King and the Struggle for Civil and Human Rights: An Enduring Legacy: In Memoriam." *The Journal of African American History* 92:1 (January 2007): 106–17.

NEWSPAPERS AND MAGAZINES

@Issue Section. "The Death of Martin Luther King, Jr.: 40 Years Later." *Atlanta Journal-Constitution* (March 30, 2008): F1-7.

Applebome, Peter. "Coretta Scott King, 78, Widow of Dr. Martin Luther King, Jr. Dies." *The New York Times* (January 31, 2006), www.nytimes.com/2006/01/31/national/31cnd-coretta.html.

Auchumutey, Jim. "We Lost a Hero But Kept the Peace." *Atlanta Journal-Constitution* (March 30, 2008): A1, A10.

Burns, Rebecca. "The Remarkable Behind-the-Scenes Story of King's Funeral: An Oral History." *Atlanta Magazine* (April 2008): 96–105, 144–48.

"Coretta Scott King: Commemorative." *Atlanta Journal-Constitution* (February 7, 2006).

Gentry, Mae. "In the Words of Coretta King." *Atlanta Constitution* (January 20, 2002): C1, C8.

Gentry, Mae. "I Feel Really Good." *Atlanta Constitution* (January 15, 2004), C1, C6.

Posner, Howard. "Coretta King Married the Man and His Vision." *Atlanta Constitution* (January 16, 1986), 1A, 8A.

Pomerantz, Gary. "Interview: Coretta Scott King: 'I Have Never Been Just a Symbol.'" *Atlanta Constitution* (January 17, 1993), A1, A12.

Towns, Hollis R. "Capturing *Her* Dreams." *Atlanta Journal-Constitution* (July 21, 1996),

ENCYCLOPEDIA ARTICLES

"Coretta Scott King." *Encyclopedia Britannica*. 2008. Online Library Edition. http://library.eb.com/eb/article-9002849.

"Coretta Scott King." *King Encyclopedia*. The King Papers Project. http://www.stanford.edu/group/King/about_king/encyclopedia/king_coretta_scott.htm.

McCarty, Laura T. "Coretta Scott King (1927–2006)." *The New Georgia Encyclopedia*, published June 6, 2007. Available at http://www.georgiaencyclopedia.org/nge/article.jsp?id=h-2519&sug=y

Uffelman, Minoa D. "Coretta Scott King." *The Encyclopedia of Alabama*, published March 13, 2008. Available at http://eoa.auburn.edu/face/Article-Printable.jsp?id=h-1489.

WEB SITES

"Coretta Scott King: Pioneer of Civil Rights." *The Academy of Achievement: A Museum of Living History*. http://www.achievement.org/autodoc/page/kin1int-1.

"Coretta Scott King Book Awards." *American Library Association*. http://www.ala.org/ala/emiert/corettascottkingbookaward/corettascott.cfm.

"Coretta Scott King Interview with Tavis Smiley." *The Tavis Smiley Show*. January 17, 2005. http://www.pbs.org/kcet/tavissmiley/archive/200501/20050117.html.

Lohr, Kathy. "Coretta Scott King Honored as Champion of Civil Rights." *National Public Radio*. February 7, 2006. http://www.npr.org/templates/story/story.php?storyId=5180053.

Martin Luther King, Jr. Center for Nonviolent Social Change. http://www.thekingcenter.org.

INDEX

About the Author

LAURA T. McCARTY is vice president of the Georgia Humanities Council. She serves as state coordinator for National History Day in Georgia and she wrote a variety of articles for the *New Georgia Encyclopedia*. She also is a member of the advisory committee for the Georgia Center for the Book.